A Scandal in Königsberg, 1835–1842

A Scandal in Königsberg, 1835–1842

CHRISTOPHER CLARK

ALLEN LANE
an imprint of
PENGUIN BOOKS

ALLEN LANE

UK | USA | Canada | Ireland | Australia
India | New Zealand | South Africa

Allen Lane is part of the Penguin Random House group of companies
whose addresses can be found at global.penguinrandomhouse.com.

Penguin Random House UK
One Embassy Gardens, 8 Viaduct Gardens, London SW11 7BW

penguin.co.uk

First published in Great Britain by Allen Lane 2025

001

Copyright © Christopher Clark, 2025

Penguin Random House values and supports copyright.
Copyright fuels creativity, encourages diverse voices, promotes freedom
of expression and supports a vibrant culture. Thank you for purchasing
an authorized edition of this book and for respecting intellectual property
laws by not reproducing, scanning or distributing any part of it by any
means without permission. You are supporting authors and enabling
Penguin Random House to continue to publish books for everyone.
No part of this book may be used or reproduced in any manner for the
purpose of training artificial intelligence technologies or systems. In accordance
with Article 4(3) of the DSM Directive 2019/790, Penguin Random House
expressly reserves this work from the text and data mining exception.

The moral right of the author has been asserted

Set in 12/14.75pt Dante MT Std
Typeset by Six Red Marbles UK, Thetford, Norfolk
Printed and bound in Great Britain by Clays Ltd, Elcograf S.p.A.

The authorized representative in the EEA is Penguin Random House Ireland,
Morrison Chambers, 32 Nassau Street, Dublin D02 YH68

A CIP catalogue record for this book is available from the British Library

ISBN: 978–0–241–76788–7

Penguin Random House is committed to a sustainable future
for our business, our readers and our planet. This book is made from
Forest Stewardship Council® certified paper.

In memory of Jonathan Steinberg (1934–2021)

Contents

1. The City of Almost — 1
2. News from Königsberg — 12
3. The Prophet of the Pregel — 23
4. Ida's Awakening — 38
5. Varieties of Religious Understanding — 46
6. The Difficult Ascent of Johann Ebel — 56
7. The Ebelians — 62
8. Charge and Counter-Charge — 72
9. Building a Case — 77
10. The Trial Begins — 83
11. Diestel Testifies — 89
12. A Media Sensation — 96
13. Dr Sachs Accuses — 102
14. The End of the Road — 116
15. Closing Thoughts — 126

Notes — 153
Acknowledgements — 175
List of Illustrations and Photo Credits — 177

Between 1835 and 1842, scandal tightened around two clergymen in the Baltic port city of Königsberg. It destroyed their reputations, drove them out of their jobs and into prison, and banished them from public life. Their legal exoneration of the most serious charges against them came too late to reverse the damage. I have been thinking about this small vortex of turbulence ever since I happened on the relevant files in the early 1990s. The campaign of denunciations and rumour that took down the Lutheran preachers Johann Ebel and Heinrich Diestel belongs to an age before the advent of paparazzi, radio, television and digital social media, but that is precisely what endows their story with fabular power. Resemblances to present-day persons and situations, though not intended, cannot be ruled out.

1.

The City of Almost

In the 1830s, the city of Königsberg still bathed in the amber glow of the late Enlightenment, at least in the minds of educated people who had never been there. Immanuel Kant (1724–1804) had lived, studied, written and taught here for most of his life, the clocklike regularity of his daily routines attracting small crowds of gawpers. His remains lay in the professors' crypt of the city's cathedral and a monument consisting of a bust by Johann Gottfried Schadow on a plinth of grey Silesian marble stood in the main lecture theatre of the university. The former house and garden of the great man had been taken over by a bathing facility, but the new owner of the house had fixed a marble tablet above the door with the inscription: 'Immanuel Kant lived and taught here from 1783 until 12 February 1804'.[1] All three sites counted among the city's principal tourist destinations.

The intricate geography of the city was etched into the memory of at least some by the 'Königsberg Bridge Problem', one of the world's most famous mathematical puzzles. Seven bridges crossed the three arms of the River Pregel. Was it possible, the Swiss mathematician Leonhard Euler asked in 1735, to walk a route through the town by crossing each bridge once and only once? And if it was not, could this impossibility be mathematically proven? The 'geometry of position' Euler

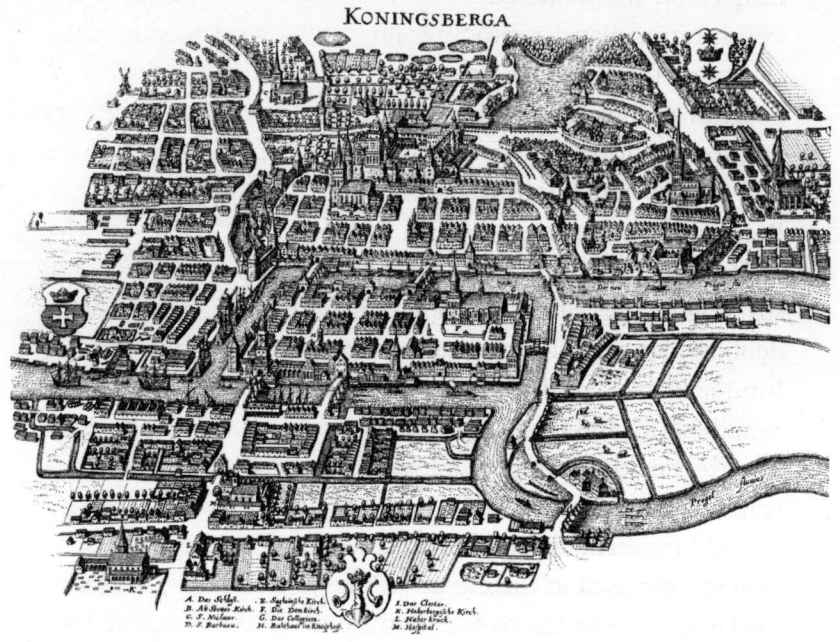

Bird's-eye plan of Königsberg, showing the seven bridges over the Pregel river, Kneiphof Island in the centre. Engraving by Matthäus Merian, 1652.

devised to prove that it was *not* possible laid the foundations of modern combinatorial topology.[2]

Königsberg was the capital city of East Prussia, the easternmost province of the Prussian kingdom. This was the provincial descendant of the Duchy of Prussia, a Baltic principality that had been controlled by the Teutonic Order until its secularization in 1525. By means of complex marital manoeuvring, the Hohenzollern Electors of Brandenburg in Berlin secured the right of succession to this far-flung territory. Seventeenth-century Ducal Prussia, which was roughly as large as Brandenburg itself, lay outside the Holy Roman

Empire on the Baltic coast, surrounded by the lands of the Polish-Lithuanian Commonwealth and subject to the sovereignty of the Kings of Poland. It was a place of windswept beaches and inlets, cereal-bearing plains, wide lakes, marshes and sombre forests. Over seven hundred kilometres of roads and tracks, virtually impassable in wet weather, lay between Berlin and Königsberg.

Only in 1657 did King John Casimir of Poland cede full sovereignty over Ducal Prussia to the Hohenzollerns of Brandenburg, an event of enormous importance for the dynasty's future. In 1701, during the reign of Elector Frederick III of Brandenburg, the Ducal Prussian sovereignty would be used to acquire the title of king for the House of Hohenzollern. In due course, even the ancient and venerable name of Brandenburg would be overshadowed by 'Kingdom of Prussia', the name increasingly used in the eighteenth century for the totality of the lands ruled by the dynasty. The peripheral location of East Prussia thus belied its centrality to the history of the kingdom. No wonder East Prussians thought of themselves as the inhabitants of a 'country' (*Land*), rather than of a province.

In the mid-nineteenth century, Prussians from across the Hohenzollern lands also remembered Königsberg as a theatre of the struggle against Napoleon and the rebirth of the Kingdom of Prussia. After the destruction of the Prussian armed forces at the hands of Napoleon in 1806–7, the court had fled to Memel on the border of the Russian Empire. Königsberg was occupied by the French army and subjected to exorbitant requisitioning and contributions. The resulting war debts would not be paid off until 1900.[3] From the autumn of 1807, the city became the headquarters of a remarkable cohort of statesmen and officials – Stein, Hardenberg, Scharnhorst, Clausewitz, Gneisenau, Wilhelm von Humboldt and Boyen, not to mention Theodor von Schön and Carl von Altenstein. These men formed the embryo of a new kind of administration, tightly organized around thematic administrative and decision-making centres, and focused on seizing the opportunities offered by the Prussian defeat in order to rationalize decision-making structures and channel the dormant energies of state and society.

It was also from here that Napoleon launched his doomed campaign against the Russian Empire. By June 1812, some 300,000 men – French, Germans, Italians, Dutch, Walloons and others – were gathered in east Prussia. It soon became clear that the provincial administration was in no position to coordinate the provisioning of this vast mass of troops. The previous year's harvest had been poor and grain supplies were quickly depleted. Hans Jakob von Auerswald, Provincial President of West and East Prussia, reported in April that the farm animals in both provinces were dying of hunger, the roads were strewn with dead horses, and there was no seed corn left. The provincial government's provisioning apparatus soon broke down under the pressure, and individual commanders simply ordered their troops to carry out independent requisitioning. It was said that those who still owned draught animals ploughed and sowed at night, so as not to see their last horse or ox carted off. Others hid their horses in the forest, though the French soon got wise to this practice and began combing the woods for concealed animals. There were numerous reports of excesses by the French troops, especially extortion, plundering and beatings. One report from a senior official spoke of devastation 'even worse than in the Thirty Years War'.[4]

Throughout the province, the mood gradually shifted from resentment to a simmering hatred of the Napoleonic forces. Vague early rumours of French setbacks in Russia were greeted with excitement and heartfelt *schadenfreude*. The first sketchy reports of the burning of Moscow (razed by the Russians to deny Napoleon winter quarters) arrived in Königsberg at the beginning of October. There was particular interest in reports of the appalling destruction inflicted on the Grande Armée by irregular forces of Cossacks and armed peasant partisans. On 14 December, the 29th bulletin of the Grande Armée put an end to any further doubts about the outcome of the Russian campaign. Issued in the Emperor's name, the bulletin blamed the catastrophe on bad weather and the incompetence and treachery of others, announced that Napoleon had left his men in Russia and was hastening westwards towards Paris, and closed with a remarkably brutal expression of imperial self-centredness: 'The Emperor's health has never been better.'

As the last stragglers of the French Grande Armée entered Königsberg on 20 December 1812, the city became the backdrop for a world-historical moment. The once-invincible army of Napoleon was a ravaged remnant of its former self. Johann Theodor Schmidt, the President of Police in Königsberg, recalled the sight of the French limping westwards out of Russia:

> The noblest figures had been bent and shrunken by frost and hunger, they were covered with blue bruises and white frost-sores. Whole limbs were frozen off and rotting [. . .] they gave off a pestilential stench [. . .]. Their clothing consisted of rags, straw mats, old women's clothing, sheepskins, or whatever else they could lay hands on. None had proper headgear; instead they bound their heads with old cloth or pieces of shirt; instead of shoes and leggings, their feet were wrapped with straw, fur or rags.[5]

The slow-burning anger of the peasantry now ignited into acts of revenge as the rural population took matters into their own hands. 'The lowest classes of the people,' District President Theodor von Schön reported from Gumbinnen, 'and especially the peasants, permit themselves in their fanaticism the most horrific mistreatment of these unhappy wretches [. . .] in the villages and on the country roads, they vent all their rage against them [. . .]. All obedience to the officials has ceased.'[6]

For several weeks it seemed that the French might be intending to defend the walled city of Königsberg against the pursuing Russians, a decision that would have exposed the city to bombardment and devastation – this was an era in which the populations of besieged cities often paid a terrible price for their refusal to submit. But at ten o'clock in the evening of 4 January 1813, as the skies over Königsberg glowed red with the reflected light of the Russian campfires, the chief of police and his staff discovered that the French had simply disappeared from the city and stolen off westwards. By midnight, the first Cossack scouts could be seen riding quietly on unshod horses to confirm that the French had gone.[7] Königsberg now became the place where Prussia changed from being a reluctant ally of the French to a member of the coalition that would drive Napoleon and his armies out of Germany and restore the integrity and independence of Prussia. It was here on 5 February 1813 that the East Prussian Estates, widely known at the time as 'representatives of the nation', convened under a Russian interim occupation to take control of the new situation. Contemporaries experienced and remembered these events as a new point of departure in the history of the kingdom.

Yet for first-time visitors in the 1830s, the experience of arriving in Königsberg was usually a disappointment. Since 1828,

'Reichsstraße Nr. 1' had connected Berlin with Königsberg via 565 kilometres of government-built all-weather roads. The 'Express Mail Coach', introduced on this route in 1821, could cover this distance in only five or six days. (Not until 1857, when the railway link was completed, did it become possible to make the journey in one day.) The sight that greeted weary travellers as they descended from their coaches was not especially inspiring. There were seven gates in the city walls. These were not objects of great beauty and most of them, a contemporary noted, were 'of mediocre construction'. There had been plans afoot since 1834 to demolish and rebuild the Sackheim Gate through which Prussian troops had passed in 1813 to join the struggle against France; this would have supplied the city with at least one presentable entrance, but as late as 1840 work on the proposed improvements had not yet begun.[8] Even friends of the city conceded that it lacked distinguished public and private buildings. There were no splendid residences in the style of Potsdam and Berlin.[9] And the houses of Königsberg were narrow. 'Most of them,' wrote one son of the city, 'are only three windows wide; indeed I know of a few which are only one window in breadth' – in such houses, he added, 'there is never enough light'.[10]

The finest houses could be found along the Langgasse, but their colours and design were too varied to compose an attractive streetscape. The thoroughfares of the East Prussian capital had once been quite broad, but thanks to lax building regulations almost every property owner in the central districts had filled the space in front of his house with a staircase, an outbuilding, or some other structure, so that by the beginning of the nineteenth century, only the middle part of the street, which was just wide enough for two carriages, was still free. The first purpose-built paved footpath was laid in 1816 on the Fließstraße, but it was a long time before other streets received the same treatment.[11] Pedestrians were forced to walk in the deep muck and dung stirred up by so many vehicles and often found themselves in mortal danger, because there was nowhere to take shelter when two carriages happened to pass each other. The various sheds and porticos gave such a messy and chaotic general impression, one citizen reported, that he could scarcely believe he was walking on the main streets of a major European city.[12]

The most disappointing feature of all was the riverfront. Everyone agreed that the city was well situated on a fine, broad river that almost never flooded. The River Pregel approached the city in two parallel arms that in joining formed an island, known as the Kneiphof, which was an almost perfect extended rectangle. The river's right bank rose gently and from several pretty ponds there flowed streams whose strong current drove many mills. The quay along the Pregel could have been one of the finest in Germany if the houses along it had not been built with their rear ends, 'which are even uglier than the fronts', facing towards the water. To make matters worse, the banks of the watercourse were not lined with stone quays or tiled embankments but secured with wooden stakes. The rotten, wet wooden palisades along the Pregel struck an unhappy contrast with the stately quays of the Spree in Berlin or the Seine in Paris. The suburbs of Königsberg were better laid out, because there were fewer outhouses and obstructions, but they were also scrappy and chaotic, with streets running between the picket fences of gardens and many individual patches of unbuilt space, even on the main thoroughfares. 'One could find awful hovels between some of the finest buildings'.[13]

None of this meant that the city lacked charm. It just meant that the best views of Königsberg were not of the city itself but from its houses and bridges onto the river or into the surrounding countryside. The Pregel was the true commercial heart of Königsberg. The waters around the islanded Kneiphof were filled in spring and summer with numerous ships. Natives and visitors alike took pleasure in picking out the Baltic trade vessels of the Swedes, the English and the Dutch. Then there were the Polish *wicine*, flat-bottomed mastless river barges up to 170 feet in length that worked the northern rivers. Many of these craft were seasonal visitors, but a portion of them remained over winter, resting along the banks of the Pregel.

In summer, the streets were full of people boarding or alighting from the ships: Polish noblemen, commoners and Jews; Russians and Swedes in national dress. One could hear Latvian in the Rossgarten, Lithuanian in the Sackheim district, Polish on the Ox Market, Russian in the Vorstadt district, and Dutch, English,

View of the Green Bridge over the Old Pregel River, with the Stock Exchange and the tower of the Green Gate to the right of it. Note the masts of ships in Königsberg's harbour in the distance. Print published by W. Barth, c.1810.

Swedish and Danish at the Licent on the northern bank of the Pregel just east of the Kneiphof. (The Licent was the Licence Packing House where people arriving by ship deposited their suitcases and packages.) From the Green Bridge on the southwestern corner of the Kneiphof there was a magnificent view downriver towards the Dutch Barrier through a forest of masts – in winter one could observe countless walkers and sledges out on the ice. From the Dutch Barrier westward towards the Baltic, there were marvellous views at sunset, when the waters of the Pregel became a carpet of rippling gold. From the upper storeys of the houses of the Sackheim district one could see the ships arriving from Lithuania and the flatlands behind them. From parts of the Rossgarten one could see westward down the curves of the river all the way to the coast at Pillau.

The presence of Immanuel Kant at the city's university, known as the Albertina, had once attracted to the city many talented young people who wanted to acquire an understanding of the latest philosophical trends. But after his death in 1804 at the age of seventy-nine, the university lapsed into the status of a sleepy provincial college. In the years 1802–5 the average number of enrolled students was only 132. Even after extensive reforms to the curriculum and the establishment of new clinics and research facilities, the number of students never exceeded 452. The political tone of student life was muted by the standards of the German cities of this era.[14] The professoriate included some moderately distinguished figures, such as the lively Hegelian philosopher Karl Rosenkranz, and these individuals were well known in the city, but before 1848 there were no living figures of global renown. In a sketch of his adoptive city published in 1842, Rosenkranz, who had lived there for nine years, captured Königsberg's status as one of the lesser lights of the German-speaking world:

The City of Almost

A mocking wit might say of Königsberg that it is the city in which everything exists in a state of almost. It is almost a royal residence; dukes used to live here, electors and kings too, on occasion. It is almost an industrial city, for it has several large factories. It is almost a seaside city, because two- and three-masted ships can reach the centre of town, though the actual harbour is Pillau, seven miles away. It is almost a wealthy city because it has a number of prosperous merchants. It almost has a fortress, because a small fort on the Holländer Damm is at least called 'fortress' – and so on and so forth . . .[15]

Königsberg was a world of small distances, easily covered on foot, where almost everyone knew almost everyone. Johann Wilhelm Ebel, a preacher at the Old City Church, was hailed by parishioners and former school pupils whenever he walked in the streets, and everyone knew the burly preacher and division chaplain Heinrich Diestel of the Haberberg Church, who strode through town 'like a Hussar commander'.[16]

2.
News from Königsberg

There was nothing to please Carl Sigmund Franz Freiherr vom Stein zum Altenstein in the report from Königsberg. Almost everything in it was alarming and unpleasant.[1] A bizarre sect, influenced by the esoteric teachings of a dead eccentric, had taken root at the heart of the city's religious life. The leader, a preacher by the name of Ebel, had encouraged his followers to engage in gross sexual impropriety. Women played a prominent role in these aberrations, many of them daughters of the province's most prestigious families. There was talk of a pregnancy out of wedlock; two young women had apparently died of exhaustion caused by excessive arousal. The author of the report was Theodor von Schön, President of the Province of Prussia, a long-standing acquaintance of the minister and one of the great political personalities of the kingdom.

In the summer of 1835, when the letter arrived, Altenstein had been in post in Berlin as the Minister of Church Affairs for eighteen years. His was a key position in the Prussian cabinet. With a total of twenty senior officials, this was one of the kingdom's larger ministries. It straddled a strategically important bundle of responsibilities. The full title was the Ministry of Clerical, Educational and Medical Affairs, but contemporaries usually called it the Kultusministerium – *Kultus* referring both to religion and to culture, which also fell under Altenstein's remit.[2]

Altenstein had lasted so long in this job – the average tenure for a person in his post over the lifespan of the ministry (1817–1934) was five years – because he had earned a reputation as a safe pair of hands. He was a reformer by political instinct. In the winter of 1804–5 he had attended lectures by the philosopher Johann Gottlieb Fichte on 'The Foundations of the Age'. From these and other readings in Fichte's works, Altenstein extracted a belief in the fundamentally progressive character of history, its movement towards ever better states of affairs.³ When disaster struck Prussia in the form of defeat at the hands of Napoleon in 1806, he was among those who saw the chance for a re-founding of the Prussian state. The 'Riga Memorandum' of 1807, which Altenstein helped to formulate, proposed a sweeping renovation of the state structure whose purpose was to unleash the forces latent in the Prussian economy and society. Aristocratic and corporate privilege should be pruned back, markets deregulated, and the administration opened to merit and talent. If the state were to survive the forces awakened by the French Revolution, it must absorb them as motors for its own renewal. Among the prerequisites for this renewal, Altenstein argued, was a strong and cohesive administration with an activist consciousness of its calling.⁴

But if the minister was a reformer, he was also a man of balance and circumspection. As a person of noble title but of modest private means, he had always steered close to the sources of official patronage. He believed deeply in authority. Only a strong monarchy could govern well. 'In a monarchical state,' he wrote, 'it is indisputably best if the king himself governs, providing he at least possesses the basic prerequisites for this role.'⁵ The objective of reform was to synchronize the energies of a liberated civil society with the progressive objectives of the state. The French Revolution had shown that clutching onto an obsolete political system would lead to total

Carl Freiherr vom Stein zum Altenstein, 1826. Lithograph by Emil Krafft.

destruction. The state had to remain nimble. But it was possible to bring about orderly transformations if wise and moderate heads could be found to guide them. Administration, by this reading, was a process of controlled upheaval.

Throughout his adult life, Altenstein had always steered towards the political centre. When, in the 1790s, a fight broke out in his native Ansbach between protectionists and free traders, he manoeuvred pragmatically between them, adopting measures that combined elements of both positions. After the conservative crackdown of 1819, when the Prussian government and the states of the German Confederation came down hard on radical student networks, Altenstein objected to measures that would limit the freedom of the universities from censorship. He was also supportive of the freedom of academic research. When two philologists at the University of Berlin, who had just returned from a research trip to Paris, were accused by police spies of having met with dangerous revolutionaries in Strasbourg, Altenstein shielded them from punitive action and intervened to ensure that their good name was restored. He defended liberal colleagues against the machinations of conservatives in the government.[6]

On the other hand, he objected when the rationalist theological faculty in Berlin claimed that it was unable to examine the doctoral dissertation of the conservative young evangelical Friedrich Tholuck, and he later supported the candidacy of Tholuck for the post vacated by the radical theologian Wilhelm Martin Leberecht de Wette after the 1819 crackdown. So Altenstein was also prepared to correct for the biases of the progressive side. He was the minister who, in 1818, secured the philosopher Georg Friedrich Wilhelm Hegel to fill the academic vacancy at the University of Berlin created by Fichte's death four years earlier. In the letter he wrote explaining the case for Hegel's appointment, Altenstein found words that eloquently characterized his own course as a public figure:

> There is a very great difficulty right now in finding a university teacher for the discipline of philosophy who, being equidistant from paradoxical, attention-grabbing, unsustainable systems and from political or religious prejudices, teaches his science with wisdom and equanimity.

If Hegel was the man for the job, this was because 'he is as far from religious zealotry as he is from unbelief'.[7]

As this last remark suggests, Altenstein also followed a middle course in religious affairs, the core policy domain of his ministry. This meant pushing back both against the desiccated rationalism that prevailed at many theology faculties, a frame of mind that bordered in some cases on unbelief, and against the unruly enthusiasms that expressed themselves in evangelical awakenings and separatist conventicles. The key thing was to avoid polarizing culture wars: in a letter to the editor of the *Allgemeine Kirchenzeitung*, a theologian called Ernst Zimmermann, Altenstein warned him not to use his journal for anything that might resemble a 'declaration of war against people with different outlooks'.[8]

For this cautious inhabitant of the middle ground, the letter from Königsberg was like a museum of horrors. It did not improve on second reading. For decades, Theodor von Schön wrote, religious groups had flourished outside the official Church. Among them were gatherings whose members felt themselves mired in 'complete sinfulness', meaning that they went in for 'a lot of gnashing of teeth and were inclined to emphasize the devil'. The effects on the people involved could be profound: Schön himself knew several followers of such a group, who had 'fallen into a condition of religious madness'.[9]

A particularly vigorous and challenging growth was the group that had formed around an unlettered spiritual seeker by the name of Johann Heinrich Schönherr. At first, Schön reported, people had laughed about the teachings of this man, who concerned himself pre-eminently with cosmological questions. He taught that in the primordial nothingness that preceded creation, 'two great eggs or balls had swum about, of which one was supposedly the fire and the other the water ball'. It was the conjunction between these two balls that had supposedly brought the world and everything in it into existence. Schönherr proposed the thesis that everything in the Bible ought to be understood literally. When an acknowledged ecclesiastical authority, the former Bishop Ernst Ludwig von Borowski, challenged this view, offering as a counter-argument the words of Jesus, 'I am the vine', Schönherr placidly replied that Jesus really must be a vine.[10]

Notwithstanding the outlandishness of these teachings, Schönherr drew to himself a large and loyal following. Many of these were artisans and wharf workers who lived outside the city walls and serviced the traffic on the River Pregel, which flowed in several streams through the city and down towards Pillau, seven miles away on the Baltic coast. But Schönherr's enthusiasts, for reasons that Schön found it impossible to discern, also included 'several men of the educated classes'. Among these was Johann Wilhelm Ebel, then a young theologian, now preacher at the Old City Church. Ebel, Schön reported, went much further than his mentor had ever done, and soon gathered a large society around himself. 'Scholars, clergymen and men from the first families of the land' flocked to him. Women in particular were attracted to his teachings.[11]

Within a few years, the group around Ebel began to show signs of instability. Professor Ludwig Wilhelm Sachs, the city's best-known physician and the author of well-known studies on the medical vocation and the therapeutic use of opium, was among those who attached himself to Ebel. But he later left the circle under a cloud, along with the theologian Professor Hermann Olshausen and the landowner Count Finck von Finckenstein. The defectors, who soon formed their own secessionist group, shared Ebel's belief in humankind as the instrument of God, but they were put off by the speculative talk of water and fire that Ebel had drawn from the teachings of Schönherr, and they began to suspect that Ebel regarded himself as a special mediator between Christ and man. From around spring 1833, Schön wrote in his report to Altenstein, the antipathies deepened and began to eat into the private and social lives of some of the key participants. Conflicts between women and men were particularly common. Schön reported that two female adherents of the group had tried to eject their husbands from their house; in a third family, the wife, a member of the circle, walked out on her husband, and in a fourth, 'a female Ebelian denounced her brother in such terms that she threatened to drive him from house and home'. 'In short: there was great upheaval in our families.'[12]

By the summer of 1835, when Schön wrote his letter, things had already come to a head. In January, Count Finckenstein learned that his cousin, Miss Zelina von Mirbach, who lived twenty miles from Königsberg on a country estate with her mother, had been 'seduced' into joining the Ebelian circle. He warned her against it in a letter. She wrote back, asking him to explain and justify his misgivings. Finckenstein responded in a letter full of accusations. It seemed that Ebel had issued instructions to engage in sexual vices so stimulating as to have caused the death of two young girls. Even more hair-raising was the moral preaching of the circle. The Ebelians, Finckenstein claimed, believed that sexual intercourse between 'sanctified' members of the movement was free of sin, and that the copulation of water and fire balls – by implication women and men – was a good thing that could only lead to a deeper understanding of the nature of the primordial beings. 'The matter is so repellent, so horrifying,' Schön wrote, 'that one can hardly find words enough to express one's disgust.'[13]

Rather than following the count's advice, Zelina von Mirbach showed his letter to Pastor Heinrich Diestel of the Haberg Church, a close friend and associate of Ebel. Diestel, a more choleric personality than the mild-mannered Ebel, was goaded to high fury by Finckenstein's accusations against his friend. He sent the count a thirteen-page letter seething with hatred in which he announced his intention to – among many other things – 'destroy and crush him as a miserable scoundrel'. Finckenstein handed the whole correspondence – including his own letter and Diestel's furious reply – over to the Criminal Court for investigation. The provincial Consistory of the Church of the Prussian Union, the most important ecclesiastical administrative body, with responsibility for the oversight and professional disciplining of the clergy, asked Finckenstein to substantiate his claims against Ebel. Diestel and Ebel now faced parallel criminal and church investigations that were likely, once they got underway, to fan further public interest and speculation.

We can't know exactly what Altenstein thought as he read the lines in Schön's report. He did not keep a journal recording his feelings about incoming correspondence. But this was an era when the political elite was especially sensitive to religious disruptions. In the 1810s, 1820s and 1830s, revivalist movements across Prussia mobilized the faithful in ways that unsettled the chemistry of the official religious communities. And at the same time as these energies were bubbling up from below, the state intervened more aggressively in the confessional life of the kingdom than at any time since the seventeenth century. On 27 September 1817, King Frederick William III announced his intention to merge the Lutheran and Calvinist confessions into a single Prussian 'evangelical-Christian church', later known as the 'Church of the Prussian Union'. The king himself was the chief architect of this new ecclesiastical entity. He designed the new 'United' liturgy, cobbling together texts from German, Swedish, Anglican and Huguenot prayer books. He issued regulations for the decoration of altars, the use of candles, vestments and crucifixes. The king invested immense energy and hope in the Union. The aim was to absorb and discipline the energy given off by revivals and to stabilize the ecclesiastical fabric of Protestantism in the face of the greatly enlarged Catholic minority in the post-war Prussian state. At the heart of the unionist project was an obsessive concern with uniformity, including not just the simplification and homogenization of vestments and liturgy but also the erection of modular *Normkirchen*, standardized churches designed to be assembled from prefabricated parts and available in different sizes to suit villages and towns.[14]

A Scandal in Königsberg

Frederick William III, King of Prussia. Engraving by A. Pflugfelder after a portrait by François Gérard, 1816.

There was abundant potential here for conflict. Protestant revivalism in Prussia tended to seek expression outside the confines of the institutional Church. Some awakened Protestants openly disparaged the official confessional structures.[15] In certain Prussian rural areas, local populations refused to patronize the services of the official clergy, preferring to congregate in prayer meetings.[16] And alongside these separatist tendencies there flourished in the numerous interstices of religious belief and practice a rich variety of eccentric variations on the norm, in which the tenets of licensed dogma blended seamlessly with folk belief, speculative natural philosophy and pseudo-science. These were the hardy weeds that shot up ceaselessly between the paving stones of official religion. They fed upon the energies released by the religious revivals and on religious needs that were not being met by the official Churches.[17] Religious belief could interact with folk magic in ways that the authorities found unsettling. In a context where the practice and institutional structure of official religion were increasingly coming under state control, the boundaries between religious non-conformity and political resistance were likely to become blurred.

Every departure from the Union rite, every critique of the official Church, every attempt to conserve or reinvigorate the old Lutheran or Calvinist traditions, every potentially sectarian or separatist activity was construed as a dangerous challenge to public authority. The king himself ordered that long reports be prepared on sectarian activity in his lands. Throughout the 1820s, Altenstein kept a close eye on sectarian developments both within and beyond the borders of the kingdom – of particular interest were the Swiss valley sects of Hasli, Grindelwald and Lauterbrunn, whose adherents were said to pray naked in the belief that clothes were a sign of sin and shame. The ministry assembled lists of sectarian publications, subsidized the publication of counter-sectarian texts, and closely monitored religious groups and associations of all kinds.[18]

The scandal that shook the city of Königsberg in the mid-1830s has to be seen against this background of wildcat religious revival on the one hand and heightened official vigilance on the other. Between them, Ebel and Diestel covered two of the most numerous and important congregations of the city. The Old City Church, where Ebel preached, occupied a prominent central location with the largest congregation in the city, and served a fashionable constituency that included many noblewomen from the best families. Diestel's stamping ground, the Haberberg Church, lay in a suburb beyond the Pregel and welcomed farmers, artisans, clerks and other middling townsfolk. The two men faced charges and accusations of the most serious kind. By the summer of 1835, a media storm was already raging around them. The scandalous rumour of their outrages began to resonate across the German lands.

Between them, Ebel and Diestel covered two of the most important churches of Königsberg. On the left: The Old Old City Church (Alte Altstädtische Kirche) in which Ebel preached until 1826, when the building was condemned and demolition work began (engraving, 1820). On the right: the Haberberger Trinitatis-Kirche, where Georg Heinrich Diestel preached until his removal from office (photograph, late 19th century).

3.
The Prophet of the Pregel

As the scandal around Ebel and Diestel unfolded in 1835–6, attention focused on a curious figure who might otherwise have fallen into obscurity. In 1835, when the inquiry into the two clergymen opened, Johann Heinrich Schönherr, who had died in Königsberg in 1826, was identified as the influential mentor of Ebel's youth and the true author of the 'doctrine' or 'system' propagated within his 'sect'.

Schönherr was born in Memel (today Lithuanian Klaipėda), a garrison town near the Prussian border with the Russian Empire, in 1770. His father was a grenadier in the Prussian army, his mother a woman from Angerburg in East Prussia. When the boy turned fifteen, he was sent to Königsberg to learn a trade. But once in the city, excited by this expansion of his horizons, he began to loiter around the colleges, watching the students and professors and trying to catch the sermons and lectures of celebrated academic personalities. He dreamed of higher things than a skilled trade and spent two years hanging about the gardens and bridges of the East Prussian capital. By the age of seventeen, he had decided he ought to become a preacher.

Since he had no money of his own and none from his parents, Schönherr signed himself into one of the city's 'pauper-house schools'. These charitable institutions charged no fees and fed their pupils free of charge. For two years he tried in vain to work through books of theology and philosophy, but he lacked the temperament for systematic study. The fashionable rationalist philosophy of the day struck him as a dry and empty jargon incapable of satisfying spiritual longings. When he listened in on lectures in the same fields at the university, the professors responded to his jejune queries by recommending that he read yet more indigestible tracts. Forsaking his studies, he went wandering instead, in a manner characteristic of other restless sages of that era, to Greifswald, Rostock, and thence across northern Germany to Rinteln on the River Weser.

It was beside a pond on the banks of the Weser that Schönherr experienced the epiphany that would shape his adult life. He happened to notice waterlilies lit by the sun, floating on the water's surface. When he peered into the cool darkness beneath them he could see that their roots did not extend to the floor of the pond. With painful intensity, it struck him that these aquatic plants owed their life and vitality to light and water alone – they required (or so it seemed to him, who knew nothing of osmosis) no other nourishment. At the same time, he heard a voice speaking to him from within his own thoughts: 'As it grows, so it has grown.'

This observation led him by degrees to the belief that the entirety of creation was founded on the union of two principles, embodied in two 'primal entities' (*Urwesen*). These he imagined as opposed spheres, one of water and thus dark, the other composed of fiery light. These spheres had originally floated or wandered in primordial space, until the moment when at last they collided and merged with each other. Only then did each of the spheres acquire consciousness of its own existence, for it was, Schönherr believed, only through relations of opposition that self-knowledge was possible. Light was the vivifying male principle, water its nurturing female counterpart. These two originary beings, the supreme male and the supreme female, bound in eternal and necessary union, explained everything.[1]

Over the years, Schönherr's homespun theosophy accumulated around this revelation, supported by selective readings of scripture. God, for example, had supposedly told Moses that in the beginning the Elohim created heaven and earth. But the word 'Elohim' (gods) is a plural, and we should thus speak of more than one primordial being. If this was true, then these entities must have pre-existed the creation of the world. Schönherr dwelt at length on the pre-creational condition when the Elohim wandered about for eternities in an infinite and empty space. Of the two beings, God the fire or the light was the faster moving and therefore the stronger and more proactive. Before the world, God searched for the other primordial being in the infinity of space, in order to work together with it, to create a world and construct beings. As he moved about in this way, God, because there was nothing to oppose him, enjoyed the tranquil inner peace and the pleasant state of awareness that comes from regular movement. And while he sailed about in the nothingness, the second primordial being, too, although the weaker of the pair, did the same. Neither knew of the location or character of the other. In later years, Schönherr would describe to his disciples – almost as if he had been there – the long meandering journey of the primal entities through the abysses of space and the glorious moment of their encounter, when the strong luminal arms of the lightsphere penetrated the cool darkness of the watersphere.[2]

Over time, Schönherr's speculations added layer after layer of imagined specifics. Once contact took place, he proposed, the water-being generated a counter-pressure against the penetrating stream of fire, creating flows of energy, spherical in form, on its edges. The stronger fire-being took up its position in vertical orientation over the weaker and the primordial light thrust with its main beam ever deeper into the water-being, until the penetrating light stream, contained by the counter-effects of the water, could go no further. It began a circling movement; a concentric current of light formed, and this current (*Strömung*) was itself a spiritual being, belonging to and similar to the primordial light, with consciousness and will. The best powers of the primordial fire passed whole and undivided into it; it was saturated through and through with light, which is why it is called 'Lucifer', or light-bearer.

By and by, Schönherr imagined, the light and the water became intertwined on many levels so that something firm and earth-like began to emerge. It was in this phase, according to Schönherr, that evil was born through the fall of Lucifer. The light-powers had waned in him because the light-Eloah needed them for the further continuation of its creational work. This awakened Lucifer's envy and provoked him to resistance. Against the will of the primordial light, he kept hold of the fire he already had, and tore away as he fell those emanations of the light-Eloah that he could lay his hands on. As Satan, the opponent, he used them to found the kingdom of evil and of sin. Only thereafter did dry land and the first shoots of vegetation appear, thanks to the continuing interaction of the two primordial beings, and then at last the lights of the heavens, the fixed stars, the sun, the moon and the planets made their appearance. They all owed their origin to the repeated extensions of the arms of light. The final phase ushered in the creation of the animals and of human beings. Here, too, both primordial beings worked together, and this is why for every species of animal there is a male and a female example. Human beings too appeared in a dual form, that is to say in two sexually different types. Both were fashioned after their primordial originals, man after the first primordial being, woman after the second. In human beings, the powers of the primordial beings at last found equilibrium, and creation was complete.

Schönherr mused not only on the creational purpose of the primordial beings, but also on their shape, which he took to be that of an egg. Holy Scripture, he noted, spoke of the primordial spirit 'brooding' on something, and on what does a living being brood, if not on an egg? And since each of the two primordial beings brooded in turn over the other as they created the world through their revolutions, they must both have been egg-shaped. And this was a truth that could be derived by more than one route: if one assumed, as one must, that the primordial beings before creation had the most perfect shape, that of a sphere, and if these spheres possessed an inner mobility and energy, then the motions thereof would surely compromise the spherical shape. The inner blowing of spirit must have changed the spherical form into an extended, rounded form, so that the spiritual winds blew into the leading point. 'Who,' Schönherr asked, 'would see anything else here but the shape of an egg?' From it the orbital paths of the heavenly bodies, the form of a drop of water, indeed even the form of fire itself are developed, even if the shape of fire is 'longer and pointier, because it belongs to the stronger of the two primordial beings, and even before the creation, its shape must have been somewhat extended, given its greater speed'.[3]

That Schönherr succeeded in securing an enthusiastic following was in part an effect of his eccentric charisma. He had, in the words of the Königsberg theologian Hermann Olshausen, who knew him well for a time:

... an eminent personality, whose resonance was greatly heightened by his costume. [. . .] His physiognomy was noble, his eyes radiant. [. . .] A long black beard flowed down as far as the belt, and the curly hair on the sides of his head was also grown to a great length. A long gown, oriental in style and a broad-brimmed hat completed the image of this unusual man.[4]

Schönherr was not the only eccentric sage to acquire a following in the Germany of these tumultuous years. 'Turnvater' Friedrich Ludwig Jahn, father of the gymnastics movement, though much better known and more important, was an analogous figure. Jahn, too, was an epic wanderer who sported 'old-German' clothes of exotic appearance, designed by himself. His lifestyle was unconventional – at various points in his wandering phase he lived in caves. Jahn and Schönherr represented a form of activism in which the project on offer to potential followers was performed by, and embodied in, the person of the charismatic teacher.

In proposing that he could construct an entire cosmology out of an imaginative encounter with some waterlilies, Schönherr displayed a confidence in the power of momentary insight that was ambient in the Königsberg of his youth. In the Preface to the second edition of his *Critique of Pure Reason* (1787), Immanuel Kant had written that he hoped in this work to 'do just what Copernicus did in attempting to explain the celestial movements'. 'When he [Copernicus] found that he could make no progress by assuming that all the heavenly bodies revolved around the spectator,' Kant wrote, 'he reversed the process and tried the experiment of assuming that the spectator revolved, while the stars remained at rest.'[5] Schönherr's revelation was fundamentally different in kind, not a change of analytical perspective but a moment of heightened awareness that led him somewhat obscurely from a single circumscribed observation to an all-embracing cosmological vision. Nevertheless, it exemplified what Schönherr, an admirer of the philosopher, doubtless felt to be an analogous moment of transformative insight leading to a fundamental break with the previous state of understanding. Like Kant, Schönherr claimed to be leading his followers out of the circular speculations of metaphysics onto the sure path of a 'science' grounded both in scripture and in observation of the natural world.

There were other local antecedents: Johann Gottfried Herder, born 1744 in Mohrungen, East Prussia, who studied under Kant in Königsberg in the early 1760s and later became a critic of Kantian philosophy, had also proposed to straddle the gap between naturalistic investigations, philosophy, theology and mystical insight. In his *Ideas for the Philosophy of the History of Mankind*, he insisted on a holistic and organic vision of the world, in which the forms of all living beings expressed the same universal laws, a cosmic order that could only be grasped by means of analogy, since the fullness of its intricacy and extent lay beyond the limits of human reason. Every thing was a synecdoche for everything. 'From the universe to the grain of dust, from the force that moves suns and planets to the gossamer of a spider's web, there is but one wisdom, one goodness, one power that prevails.'[6]

In the 1790s and early 1800s, Friedrich Wilhelm Joseph Schelling, too, born 1775 in Leonberg, Württemberg, mediated between the natural sciences and metaphysical philosophy in works that attempted to reconcile the fundamental unity of a divinely created world with the diversity of the forms within it. Schelling did this by positing an 'original opposition' capable of explaining how the light of the sun, for example, could be the cause of the oppositions observable on earth – heat and cold, light and dark, solid and liquid. In enigmatic formulations that resonate with Schönherr's cosmogony, Schelling speculated in a study of what he called the 'World-Soul' (*Weltseele*) on the relationship between the weightlessness of the 'Light-Being' (*Lichtwesen*) and the heaviness of matter, seeing in the bond between them the essence of all organic life. The 'totality of mass' and 'the identity of the Light-Being', he wrote, enter into a higher unity that relates with each as an attribute of itself. 'Organic life depends above upon this evolution of the bond [between light and matter], hence the endless love of every plant for light . . .'[7]

The important point here is not that Schönherr knew and read Schelling and Herder, though he almost certainly did have some knowledge of their work, but that his writings and teachings, though less sophisticated and influential than theirs, bore the imprint of the same period temperament. A follower of Schönherr would later hyperbolically defend his work – after the theosopher's death – as the 'final metamorphosis of philosophy that Schelling had called for'.[8] Contemporaries found it unremarkable that teachings of the type Schönherr offered should have appealed to the boatmen and wharf workers of the River Pregel, the glovers of the Löbenicht district, and the peasants of the outlying Königsberg suburbs. People of this sort liked, according to one account, 'to drink their beer and smoke their pipes while listening to his sermons on the Book of Revelation and on the coming of the Judgement Day'.[9] And there is nothing in their credulity that ought to surprise us, given the great numbers of people of our own time who are prepared to believe in any number of fanciful theories.

More puzzling to contemporaries was the attention Schönherr received from educated people and even from young clergymen, such as Johann Ebel. But here we should note that different people discerned different things in Schönherr's message. And how one summarized his teachings depended upon the observer's point of view. The scandal around Ebel and Diestel generated a highly polarized body of testimony in which virtually everyone sided either with Ebel and his people or against them. As one commentator on the controversy observed, there was a politics involved in the description of Schönherr's speculations.[10] Hostile observers were likely to describe them as a 'doctrine' or 'system', whereas sympathetic ones referred to the theosopher's 'teachings'. Hostile writers made great play with Schönherr's unusual appearance, especially the 'oriental' gown and the long beard worn in what one narrator described as the 'Latvian fashion'. Most accounts did not cite his few theosophical publications, on the grounds that 'their meaning [...] can only be grasped with difficulty, and the form of argument is precisely the strongest evidence for the groundlessness of the opinions advanced in them'.[11] Sceptical accounts used a naïve and concrete language to de-sophisticate the teacher's theosophical speculations: the primordial beings were 'inorganic lumps', 'light and water balls' or 'eggs' (suggesting testicles) swimming about in the darkness and 'bumping' into each other by accident. The encounter between them was described as if it were the meeting between a lascivious male flâneur and a street girl. Many commentators hinted that Schönherr saw in all sexual congress between women and men a re-enactment of this original union.[12]

Two anecdotes recur in sceptical accounts of Schönherr's life. According to the first, Schönherr was so convinced of the power of his insight that he attempted to win the allegiance of Kant. Granted an audience with the great man, Schönherr expounded with passion and candour his 'system' of the two primal entities. Kant listened patiently and replied that if all of this were true,

Long after his death, the famous philosopher remained important to the identity and reputation of Königsberg. The house of Immanuel Kant, Prinzessinstraße, Königsberg. Print by Friedrich Heinrich Bils, 1842.

then man ought in theory to be able to subsist by light and water alone, without any organic nourishment. Schönherr enthusiastically conceded the point, whereupon Kant advised him to try this method himself, with a view to adopting its success as an advertisement for the truth of his doctrine. Schönherr spent several days trying to live from light and water alone and was soon persuaded by hunger to abandon the attempt.

The second such anecdote relates to Schönherr's preoccupation in the last years of his life with the plan to construct a boat on the River Pregel in accordance with a design that had come to him in a dream. Schönherr supposed that this mystical ship would be capable of sailing against wind and tide 'without sails, oars or horses'. The vessel was eventually built with the charity of friendly merchants and the freely given labour of wharfmen affiliated with his circle, but when it was launched, it sank immediately into the mud near the bank of the river, where it remained until it was broken up.[13]

What was lost (or concealed) from view in the sceptical accounts was the diffuse intensity of Schönherr's dualist vision, its autodidactic preoccupation with the most enigmatic passages of scripture, and its pretension to the dignity of theological scholarship and natural science. Why should water and light not be the formative principles of creation, one of his followers would later ask. After all, the prophets of the old and the new covenant had spoken of God as a consuming fire. When God pronounced his fiat, 'Let there be light!', the rays of that light shone into the darkness over the depths of the water. If man were not fashioned out of water and spirit, John the Baptist would not have baptized with water, and Christ would not have descended into the River Jordan in order to 'fulfil all righteousness' (Matthew 3:15 and 3:11). There was no conflict here with the insights generated by modern science. For the natural sciences had themselves recently demonstrated not only that light was unitary (i.e. of one undifferentiated substance) but also that water was 'indivisible', as Johann Wilhelm Ritter's 'Galvanic Investigations of the Chemical Nature of Water' had supposedly proven.[14] Finally, though this is not an observation we find in contemporary discussion, it is perhaps understandable that in what we have since grown used to calling the Age of Steam a special meaning should have attached to the encounter between fire and water. Only in 1821 was the first steam engine installed in Königsberg – it was an English import, paid for by local merchants. The first steamship to be seen on the Pregel was the *Copernicus*, constructed in nearby Elbing using engines from Glasgow, which called at the city's harbour in the summer of 1828.[15] In this way, perhaps, as in many others, the religious movements of this era metabolized the innovations of modernity.

By 1822, when the Berlin government asked all district authorities to report on unauthorized religious activity in their respective areas, Schönherr had acquired a regular following. In its return for that year, the Inspectorate of Königsberg listed 'the sect of Herr Schönherr' as one of the unauthorized gatherings convening in the city. The respondent was unable to state the number of adherents, merely noting that these consisted of 'women and men, among whom there are said to be a number of schoolteachers'. Details on the teachings expounded at these gatherings were not available because these were 'kept secret'.[16]

For the young clergyman Johann Wilhelm Ebel, the power of Schönherr's teachings lay both in their cosmic explanatory scope, and in the theosopher's ability to build bridges – as Ebel saw it – between philosophy and faith. Born in 1784, Ebel hailed from Passenheim (today Polish Pasym) in Protestant, Polish-speaking Masuria, a region known for its attachment to Lutheran tradition and for its evangelical piety and sectarian enthusiasms. Various branches of the Ebel family had supplied pastors to churches in the Passenheim area for several generations and Johann Ebel grew up in a clerical household with a mystical bent.[17] Already as an adolescent he had been drawn to the Book of Psalms, the Song of Solomon, the Gospel of John and the Book of Revelation. But his father, who was himself a clergyman, counselled him against entering the ministry, on the grounds that his 'anxious [and] conscientious' character was ill-fitted to the tasks of a 'theologian of our times'.[18] It was the director of his high school who recognized the boy's aptitude for the ministry and persuaded Ebel's father to drop his objections.

The decision to leave Passenheim to study theology at Königsberg in preparation for the ministry plunged Ebel into a world suffused with a sceptical philosophical rationalism. Mockery of religion was the norm among his fellow university students and Ebel found it hard to reconcile the rationalist teachings of his instructors with the warm positive belief he had grown up with at home. He would later recall creeping back to his attic bedroom in tears after failing to counter the doubts and contradictions of teachers and fellow students. In 1802, when Ebel was eighteen years old, a friend of his family told him about a man who had found a way of bringing the entire content of the Bible into harmony with rational proofs in a manner that could shield revealed religious truth against the mockery of the sceptics. Schönherr became the mentor whose encompassing speculations offered a key to the resolution of doubt:

> Like a beam of light from heaven [Ebel would later write in a document submitted during his trial] this message lit up my heart with inexpressible pleasure; a nameless happiness took control of my entire being. All the questions inside me appeared to be answered, all the darkness was banished, and I experienced in this moment a foretaste of the fulfilment of my deepest longing.[19]

There was something emblematic in this curious alliance between a young theologian and an uneducated sage. The tension between reason and faith, between philosophy and revelation, was one of the central themes of these years. It ran like a red thread through countless clerical and intellectual biographies. For many of those preoccupied by it, this was an issue filled with urgency and pain. Resolving it was not simply a matter of establishing and defending a theoretical standpoint; it was a quest for personal equilibrium founded on a harmony between world and scripture, between liberty and grace. And Ebel was not unusual in seeking these goods from a marginal and esoteric source. In the early years following the Wars of Liberation, when the spring rain of religious revival and fashionable sentimentality stirred the dull roots of rationalist theology, it was fashionable for the 'Awakened' to frequent mystical seers and visionary nuns, to whose hermitages earnest young Protestants made long pilgrimages.

Whatever Ebel learned from Schönherr, he was himself clearly blessed with quite remarkable charismatic gifts. By the end of the Wars of Liberation, he was famous in Königsberg for the fiery oratory of his sermons and the power of the prayers with which he began and ended his religious instruction. As a man of the Awakening, Ebel cultivated a style that mixed the rough and smooth, high eloquence with moments of earthy directness. He was, as one chronicler put it, 'bold, sentimental and original, never scrupling to throw into his most solemn passages a homely phrase, an old saw, a snatch of song, even a touch of comedy, which all but forced his hearers into shouts of mirth'. A former pupil at Friedrichs College, where Ebel preached and taught for a time, recalled that his sermons had accelerated 'the unshackling of the spirit brought about by the Wars of Liberation against Napoleon'.[20]

Good looks helped too: the young Ebel wore his hair very long, so that it fell in cascades of dark curls around his neck, and he parted it down the centre of his head, 'like a lady'.[21] The writer Fanny Lewald, who attended Ebel's classes at school from the age of eight onwards, recalled a tall, slender man with 'a very fine and serious face'. 'His large dark eyes, his pale complexion and long, shiny black hair made a particular impression.' He had fine hands and when he folded them together and raised his eyes to heaven, 'he looked like an apostle'. 'One always had the impression that he spoke from the depths of his heart and to this day I am persuaded that this was the case.'[22] He possessed a sympathy for and insight into the specific predicaments of women. In 1816, this latter gift helped him to build a friendship that would shape the rest of his life.

4.
Ida's Awakening

In 1816, three years after her husband's death in battle, Ida von der Groeben still languished in a condition of profound apathy. Ida had been one of the most eligible young women of Königsberg high society. She was the third daughter of Hans Jakob von Auerswald, a senior functionary who had become President of the Province of East Prussia in 1814. Her eldest sister Lydia had married Theodor von Schön, who would succeed her father as President in 1824. The next sister, Eveline, married a wealthy nobleman by the name of Kurt von Bardeleben. Ida had many suitors but chose the handsome Count Wilhelm von der Groeben, First Lieutenant, and Adjutant in the Cuirassier Regiment 'Count Wrangel'. After his death in battle at Großgörschen on 2 May 1813, when Ida was twenty-one years old, the high spirits for which she had been renowned evaporated. She withdrew from Königsberg and lived in seclusion at the country seat of her dead husband's family.

Early nineteenth-century medical experts took a range of views on the causes and defining features of melancholy. The 'obstinate fixation of attention on one object', 'dark and confused ideas', and a tendency to develop mistaken judgements about them were identified by leading authorities as key indicators of melancholy, but protracted sadness, rumination, sleepiness, fatigue, shame, fearfulness, anxiety, despair and 'the extinction of hope' also figured in the diagnostic literature.

Grief was the most common trigger, according to one expert, but excessive dryness of the brain, cerebral change, and a shock capable of disturbing the equilibrium between the power of judgement and the power of imagination also figured in the aetiology of this disorder. The most popular treatments included bleeding, vigorous physical movement, and brushing of the back and belly – all intended to shake loose the blockages in circulation (especially of black bile) associated with the disease.

In Ida's case, the occasion of her descent into melancholy appeared, understandably enough, to be the death of her husband in battle. But her own later account of this period of illness had relatively little to say about the bereavement or its impact on her life. Instead, she dwelt on religious anxieties that had tormented her since childhood. At the heart of her disorder was the apprehension that salvation would be denied her because she had failed to find a way of loving God above all people and things: 'When I checked and discovered that I loved people – father and mother – more than God,' she wrote, 'I was filled with a great fear.' Her mother assured her that it was normal for a child to 'cling to those who were performing God's role [for her] on earth'. This comforted her for a while, but the anxiety soon returned. And underlying her fear of perdition was a deepening ontological uncertainty: Did the things around her really exist? How stable was her own existence? What relationship existed between herself and the world around her? And this incessant self-questioning was intensified by feelings of guilt about the direction of her thoughts.[1]

The problem persisted into adolescence, until the distractions of society and her own entry into 'what is known as the great world'. Ida was swept up by the fashionable romantic sensibility of her era. But if the distractions of society 'alienated [her] from the quest for the highest things', they also prevented her from finding 'true peace'. It was the death of her husband after just two years of marriage that precipitated the next phase. Only after a period of profound unhappiness, she later wrote, did her life acquire 'the direction intended by God'. Ida had never enjoyed attending church, because she found the sermons she heard there, delivered in the rationalist manner dominant at this time in the province, dry and lacking in insight. But in the preaching of Johann Ebel she found something that awakened her to a 'tense state of alertness'. The 'particular tendency of his influence,' she wrote, was 'to spread joy in the name of the Lord, to call people to joy in Him, and to freedom, to the reciprocation of his love'. This seemed 'new and unheard-of' in a time that had fallen for 'a shallow and dead religiosity'. Ebel communicated the sense of a peaceful and joyful relationship with God:

> Through Ebel's preaching I gained a glimpse into the paternal heart of God and into his love for me, of which I had hitherto had no idea, and believing in which had until now always seemed the most difficult thing. God himself soon became my true love, I felt that I had never experienced such an attachment to anyone in the whole world as I now did for him, my heavenly father, whom I now believed that I had found; aroused to joy in the deepest foundation of my soul, I had now become truly happy.[2]

When the doubts returned, and with them anxieties about her own sinfulness, Ida dared to share them with Ebel. In addition to assuring her of the mercifulness of God, the pastor urged her not to be fearful; there was a difference, he told her, between obstinate and arrogant doubts and 'an honestly searching doubt'. She should not take these thoughts too seriously, but use them for the purpose that God intended, namely as a prompt to achieve a deeper understanding of His word. When Ida saw that her fear of being condemned for the fragility of her faith was without foundation, her courage returned, at least for a time. When the fears came back, Ebel showed extraordinary patience, finding fresh insights and lines of argument every time she consulted him. 'The ordeal by fire that you are experiencing is as necessary for you as it is unintelligible from your standpoint,' he told her. 'Believe me, the Lord would rather let us sink to the gates of Hell than give us up, if we are honest. [. . .] And you are honest. You have nothing to fear. It is at night that we see the stars, just as you receive moments of insight in the heart of your struggle.'[3]

On another occasion, when Ida was overcome with the feeling that she was unreceptive to and incapable of love, she wrote to Ebel about this new assault on her peace of mind. In his response, the pastor urged her to be patient. She was right to think that she still lacked the right love. To acknowledge this was deeply humiliating, but it was also necessary and salutary. Most importantly, it was as true of Ebel himself and of all sinners as it was of Ida. But God was love, and his victory over the hearts of those who longed for him was already prepared in advance. This love had taken the form of a man precisely in order to conciliate the loveless hearts of men and women. Christians were the followers of Christ not because *they fulfilled love*, which was the law of perfection, but because *He loved them*:

> Love is the first and indispensably necessary prerequisite for redemption; it does not consist in our having loved God, but rather in the fact that he has loved us, 1 John 4. If you want to

inspect your worthiness and establish a justice, then you are on the wrong path. Therefore, I entreat and enjoin you in all seriousness in the name of the Lord do not indulge in such miscalculations, but rather let yourself enjoy grace and simply throw yourself as a death-worthy sinner into the arms of our mediator, only then will love be poured out upon you from his divine heart.[4]

Early nineteenth-century pathology acknowledged the existence of specifically religious forms of melancholy. These were conditions in which 'dark and confused conceptions' and 'sad and fearful feelings' were triggered by religious ideas and references. A tract published in 1799 claimed that of the persons confined on account of mental illness in the asylums of the German states, 'about two-thirds have become mad by way of excessive religiosity or through ruminating on religious questions'.[5] Religious melancholiacs, it was argued, exhibited certain identifying symptoms: the skin of the face might show a 'pale, yellow, earthen colour' and the eyes 'a sad, languishing, fearful gaze . . .'. The gait of melancholiacs was dawdling, the voice trembling and weak. They accused themselves of great sins and were in deep doubt as to whether they were in a state of grace. They were often disgusted by their own thoughts, which they took to be blasphemous.[6]

As for the causes, the experts offered the usual array of possible triggers, from congestion of the blood to bad air and climate, to nervous conditions and 'unfulfilled sexual desire'. Some acknowledged the possibility that melancholy could be inherited. This was relevant to Ida's case because when she informed her father of her condition, he replied: 'Not you too my poor child!' and confided in her that he had suffered from similar doubts since his youth. A persistent 'inner dissatisfaction' had left him with a strangely depressed mood which expressed itself in reclusiveness and 'an almost dark seriousness'.[7]

Mental-health experts in the early nineteenth century were reluctant to blame religion as such for the phenomenon of religious melancholy. Most of them were themselves religious in some sense or other and affirmed the role of moderate and rational forms of faith in contributing to the well-being of the individual. But they did argue that false or mistaken religious beliefs could be implicated in the journey into mental illness. Of these the most common – also identified in present-day studies of religiously motivated anxiety – was the notion that one's sins were too many and too great to be forgiven by God. Misprisions of this kind were more likely to occur, the experts argued, in religious settings marked by the rigorous policing of strict ethical injunctions or an emphasis on particular states of mind as markers of grace or perdition. If people believed that inner joy was an index of personal redemption, then some might also read their own low mood as signs of their abandonment by God and fall into a vicious circle of self-reinforcing anguish.

There was the added risk that people prone to this kind of doubt would focus on biblical passages with the potential to stir anxiety in vulnerable believers. The most important are those that refer to the 'sin against the Holy Spirit' (Matthew 12:31, Mark 3:29) for which there is no prospect of forgiveness. According to Luke 12:10, 'everyone who speaks a word against the Son of man will be forgiven, but he who blasphemes against the Holy Spirit will not be forgiven'. Since none of these passages offered any guidance on what this sin or blasphemy consisted of, there was nothing to stop anxious believers from applying it to their own behaviour or experiences. An American study of 'religious factors in mental illness' published in 1957 identified these passages as the most 'dangerous' for believers prone to anxiety, because they encouraged them to believe that they 'could not get through to God', were 'just not able to get saved', and were 'beyond the forgiveness of God'.[8]

Johann Ebel was not a pathologist, but a preacher and a pastor entrusted with the care of souls. The rationalist psychiatrist Friedrich Bird claimed to have cured a depressed young Bavarian man by confiscating his religious tracts, changing his diet, and pressing him into a regime of regular physical exercise. He told another patient that he must blame himself, and not waste his time doubting the grace of God, who no longer performed miracles. 'I asked him how he came to the idea of praying and keeping vigil as a remedy and he named me various biblical reasons. I referred him instead to earthly measures.'[9]

Ebel took a different approach. He entered deep into the logic of Ida's anxieties, meeting her on the ground of her own beliefs and intuitions, and encouraging her to reframe her experiences as encouraging prompts from God rather than signs that she had already been abandoned. There was no need for the studied 'condescension' (*Herablassung*) recommended by some pathologists as a means of winning the trust of the subject. The notion that Ida needed to learn not to love but to *be loved*, that her sense of unworthiness was not an intimation of the truth but a necessary precondition for her journey towards a fuller experience of her faith – these suggestions reveal an acute understanding of the nature of her predicament. They were aimed at providing her with the means of regaining a sense of traction: 'The fact,' Ida would later write, 'that Ebel, who knew exactly what was going on inside me, nonetheless did not pronounce a death sentence upon this illness, but allowed me to see the power of reconciliation, truly did comfort me.'[10] With time she was able to return to society and resume her place in the life of the city.

Ida's restoration to good health was a sensation. News of it passed through the elite families of Königsberg. This was a transformative moment in Ida's life, but also in that of her pastor, Dr Johann Wilhelm Ebel, who was now a famous man and a welcome guest at the homes of the province's best families.

5.
Varieties of Religious Understanding

[A pastor and three students of theology converse in a small inn on the road between Königsberg and Pillau. One of them, Manitius, has fallen asleep.]

'What do they mean, Manitius?'

Manitius opens a single eye, his mind clinging to a dream. Borcke is leaning towards him, but it's Sandemann who is speaking. In a corner near the oven sits old Pastor Gerlach from Stralsund, his chin resting on the knob of his walking stick.

'I don't know,' grunts Manitius. 'I haven't made up my mind.'

Raucous laughter from Borcke: 'He hasn't made up his mind!'

'The loaves and fishes "mean" precisely nothing, my young friends. They are what they are, they don't need to be "symbols". Our Lord wrought a miracle before the eyes of the people. It's quite simple.' It is Gerlach speaking.

Borcke throws a piece of bread into the air and catches it in his upturned hat. 'Why would God break the laws of the universe he himself created?'

'Why shouldn't he? A clockmaker is free to stop and restart his clock, or even to change its speed,' Gerlach replies. 'Who is to prevent him? God is bound by no law. He is not a constitutional monarch! Where is the constituent assembly that would bind an omnipotent creator with laws?'

'Are you saying that God is a tyrant?' quips Sandemann.

'What tyrant would lavish such riches on his subjects?' Gerlach is warming to his theme. He throws his voice as if he were preaching. 'What tyrant would leave his creatures in such liberty over themselves?'

Manitius is awake now. The last shreds of his dream have washed away.

Borcke takes the bread out of his hat and bites into it. 'But he didn't need to break the law.'

'How so?' asks Gerlach.

'This is no miracle; it is a *parable*,' Borcke explains. 'Jesus said to his disciples, bring forward all that you have and there will be enough for all. They did as he asked and – lo and behold! – there was enough. The point of the story is that if you share what you have, everyone will be better off.'

'So Jesus is an Owenite now? He wants us all to share?' Sandemann climbs gingerly onto a chair and begins to jiggle the coins in his trouser pocket. 'You are all wrong!'

'What, me too?' Manitius protests. 'I haven't even said anything yet!'

Sandemann carries on: 'Your explanations are both equally absurd. And neither can be supported from the gospel text. If this were a parable, why would the Evangelist not make that clear? He could simply write: "Everybody gave of their fish and loaves and lo! there was enough for all." But he says nothing of the sort.'

'So it *was* a miracle, then. You have proven my point!' – this from Pastor Gerlach, who has begun to warm his boots at the oven.

'Precisely not,' Sandemann retorts from atop his chair. 'Imagine the transformation of five loaves into five thousand and of two fishes into enough fish to feed a multitude. With terrifying violence, an expanding mass of bread and fish crushes the people against rocks and trees. This is not what the evangelist describes.'

'I dread to think of what is coming next, young man,' says Gerlach, his chin back on his stick.

'What's coming next is the truth!' cries Sandemann, his head bent forward under the rafters of the little inn. 'In the age of the Second Temple, the era in which the Gospels were actually written, people said of a good and beloved teacher: "He feeds his people." And our Jesus was surely a good and beloved teacher. The loaves and fishes are neither a miracle nor a parable. They are *language*, drawn from the vernacular of the age.'[1]

Just as the scandal around Ebel was breaking out in Königsberg, the world of German Protestant theology was electrified by news of a radical re-interpretation of the Gospels. *The Life of Jesus, Critically Examined* appeared in 1835–6, when its author, the theologian David Friedrich Strauss, was twenty-seven years old. Rather than reading the Gospels as revelations of divine truth, Strauss analysed them in context as historical documents and concluded that the miracles recorded in them were in fact 'myths', by which he meant not falsehoods, but forms of language used by Christ's Jewish contemporaries to exalt him. In Strauss's reading, myth became a tool for subjecting gospel revelation to an historical critique that embedded Jesus in the semantic and folkloric world of Second Temple Judaism. This was not an additive venture, intended to deepen or enrich an existing interpretation – Strauss believed that he had comprehensively discredited both orthodox and rationalist readings of the New Testament.

It is difficult today to imagine the anger and outrage stirred by this book among conservative Christians – the reception in the Islamic world of Salman Rushdie's *Satanic Verses*, though much more violent, conveys a sense of the book's impact. Within weeks of the publication of *The Life of Jesus, Critically Examined*, Strauss was sacked from his post at the Tübingen seminary and theologians across the German faculties vied with each other to condemn it. In 1839 the news that the radical-dominated Great Council of Zurich had decided to appoint Strauss to the chair of theology at the city's university triggered a culture war across the province. Conservative provincial Protestants mobilized 'committees of faith' that soon became insurrectionary organizations. A petition demanding that the appointment be annulled was presented to the electors of every parish. 'There are moments in the life of states,' declared the petitioners, 'when the legal authorities exceed their powers, and the people rise up and punish these infractions!'[2] Amidst frenzied campaigning, 39,225 electors – virtually the entire enfranchised population – voted for the petition; only 1,048 voted against it. Alarmed by the depth of the backlash, the Great Council rescinded its offer of a professorial chair and pensioned Strauss off instead.

But it was too late to stop the unrest from spreading. The organizers of the campaign were furious when they saw that the defenders of Strauss on the Great Council had no intention of resigning their offices. Preacher-agitators whipped rural parishes into a frenzy against the capital. Led by clergymen and singing hymns, columns of armed men marched on Zurich and drove out the members of the executive council. Johannes Jakob Hegetschweiler, a widely admired physician renowned for his publications on alpine vegetation, was shot in the head as he tried to mediate between the council and the insurgents; he died three days later. The *Züriputsch*, as the event came to be known, marked the entry of the Swiss-German word *putsch*, meaning a blow or a collision, into the modern political lexicon.[3]

The different ways of being religious became more and more

The *Züriputsch* revealed the explosive potential in differences of religious opinion and sentiment. Confrontation on the Paradeplatz, Zurich, between the Radicals and the Conservatives, on 6 September 1839. Print by J. W. Bachmann.

unlike each other in the decades after 1815. This was a domain in which the French Revolution and its Napoleonic aftermath had wrought especially deep transformations. As it radicalized in the early 1790s, the Revolution brought a wave of secularizing reforms directed against the wealth, privilege and power of the *ancien régime* Church. A sequence of laws stipulating the confiscation of the Church's lands in France culminated in the Civil Constitution of the Clergy, passed in Paris on 12 July 1790, which effected the complete subordination of the Church to the French revolutionary secular state. The Civil Constitution was the 'fatal moment' in the history of the Revolution; it 'marked the end of national unity and the beginning of civil war'.[4] A profound schism opened up between those prepared to accept the new order and those determined to resist it.

Varieties of Religious Understanding

From the beginning, the struggle between Catholics and secularizers broke the boundaries of the new French nation state. The French went abroad bearing a reputation for 'militant godlessness'; conversely, religion became deeply intertwined with counter-revolution across the continent.[5] And since the pope himself, Pius VI, was not just a priest, but also the elected sovereign of an Italian state commanding a small army, he was himself drawn into the struggle. The 'multi-layered actorness' of the Holy See – as a state, a diplomatic entity and the presidency of a transnational Church[6] – made it inevitable that there would eventually be a direct confrontation between Paris and Rome. In Italy and Austria, major insurrections against the French or their proxies coincided with miraculous appearances of the Virgin Mary. Priests helped to organize resistance to the French occupation in the Rhineland and in Belgium, where they coordinated boycotts of the elections called by the French authorities.[7] In the Kingdom of Italy, hostile clergy, 'fomented by the court of Rome', encouraged and on occasion even organized anti-conscription protests.[8]

As these examples show, the disruptive power of new regimes had an ambivalent impact on the Catholic Church. It represented an unprecedented assault on the wealth and political privileges of the institution. But at the same time, it catapulted many clergymen into positions from which they could exercise moral authority of a different kind. The chastened post-Napoleonic Church proved more adept at capturing and channelling the energies of popular revival than its *ancien régime* predecessor ever had. And after decades of aggressive state interventions, the new forms of Catholic revival that swept the continent after 1815 were more 'ultramontane' and less respectful of the pretensions of secular states. Ultramontanes were those who argued that the strict subordination of the Church to papal authority was the best way of protecting it from state interference (the pope being south of the Alps and thus *ultra montes* or 'beyond the mountains'). By definition, the rise of ultramontanism led to increasing tension between Catholics and state authorities. In Bavaria, a dispute broke out in 1831 over the education of children in Catholic–Protestant mixed marriages. The ultramontanes went on the offensive, and liberal publicists depicted the debate as a struggle between the forces of darkness and light. Six years later, as the scandal around Ebel and Diestel was coming to a head, a much more serious fight broke out over the same issue in Prussia, in the course of which the authorities arrested and imprisoned the ultramontane Archbishop of Cologne. Catholic Cologne, in Prussia's westernmost Rhineland Province, was a world away from Lutheran Königsberg in the kingdom's far east. But the heightening of Protestant–Catholic tensions made the authorities in all the Prussian regions nervous. Above all, it reinforced the importance of disciplining and unifying the Protestant confessional landscape.

The resulting estrangement was especially deep across the great denominational divides. The dramatic growth of culturally conservative Catholic revivals in western Europe filled liberal Protestants with fastidious horror because it suggested that the world-historical wheels of the Protestant revelation were being thrown into reverse. But it wasn't just Catholics and Protestants whose beliefs and practices made less and less sense to each other. Cracks opened on both sides of the confessional divide. There was a world of difference between the ardent, papally focused devotional culture of ultramontane Catholics and the popular piety of many Catholic leftists in France, for whom Christ was a politically radical proletarian liberator. The 'German Catholic' movement, founded in Leipzig in 1845, called for a severing of ties with Rome and a movement of enlightened spiritual renewal that would abandon traditional dogma and create the foundation for a German 'national Church' in which both Catholics and Protestants could thrive. Within two years, the movement acquired 250 congregations with a total membership of some 60,000, of whom about 40,000 were radical Catholics and 20,000 converts from Protestantism. There were close ties with Germany's leading political radicals.

The Protestants, too, experienced this disjuncture. What counted at the gatherings of evangelical Christians was the visceral experience of spiritual rebirth, not the supposedly anodyne rituals of the state Church with its rationalist clergy. Christians of this type preferred bible-reading circles and 'conventicles' to church services; the pietist noblemen who led them were joined by circles of pious artisans, labourers and peasants, who knelt in fields to hear sermons from spiritually inspired shepherds. And while this reorientation towards mystery and miracle was taking place at the evangelical end of the Protestant spectrum, rationalist theologians were purging their Christianity of much of its traditional content: from miracles and prophecies to the doctrine of original sin, the existence of hell and the divinity of Christ. The Protestant movement known as the 'Friends of Light' (*Lichtfreunde*) combined rationalist theology with a presbyterial-democratic organizational culture in which authority was devolved down to the individual congregation and its elected elders. The movement was particularly successful in attracting poor urban and rural artisans, especially in Saxony, the most industrialized state in the German Confederation.

Moreover, as they became less intelligible to each other, these divergent forms of religious sentiment and behaviour became intertwined with political antagonisms. For

Catholic ultramontane conservatives repelled by the secularizing impacts of the French Revolution or the July Revolution of 1830, liberal Catholics were the bastard offspring of a perverted reason and people with whom there could be no pacts or compromises. For some radical commentators on religion, enthusiasm of the evangelical type was virtually indistinguishable from mental illness. In the diagnoses of radical pathologists, empirical observation could mesh with rationalist hostility to supposedly excessive and irrational forms of religion.[9] It was no wonder, the physician Gustav Blumröder wrote in 1837, that religious madness was especially common among the members of Protestant conventicles, since these were bastions of 'senseless rigorism and terrorism', in which 'narrow-minded but well-meaning fanatics [. . .] gruesome, deliberate stupifiers, theological half-men' ensnared susceptible victims.[10]

In the early nineteenth century, religion passed like a spiritual power surge across Europe, threatening on occasion to burn out the grid. It energized the European archipelago of political commitments, generating endless new combinations. The new combinations were possible because the shocks of the revolutionary era had shaken religion partly loose from the institutions of theological and ecclesiastical authority, allowing it to flow out into the world. The waning of ecclesiastical authority went hand in hand with an expansion of religious feeling. The consequence was a loss of certainty and a proliferation of possibilities.

The deep fissures in religious life help to explain the swift escalation of the scandal around Johann Ebel from 1835. Public opinion was easily aroused by controversies around religious questions, as the insurrection triggered by the appointment of David Friedrich Strauss would later show. The widening of the spectrum of religious options – from ultra-rationalists at one end to pietism and separatist groupings at the other – encouraged hyperbole. Ebel's followers saw the liberal worthies who campaigned against him as the exponents of a spiritless and merely nominal Christianity motivated by a political hostility to revealed religion. In the eyes of his progressive detractors, Ebel was the negation of reason itself; he was the champion of darkness, fanatical zeal and ignorance against tolerance and progress.

6.
The Difficult Ascent of Johann Ebel

Johann Ebel was twenty years old when he passed his exams at the Theology Faculty of the University of Königsberg in 1804 and received his licence to preach. For the moment, his chief task was supervising the studies of the sons of the Imperial Burgrave zu Dohna at Schlobitten, one of the great magnate families of East Prussia – an earlier example of the affiliation with prestigious patrons that would shape his career. It was Dohna who in 1806 offered Ebel a place as preacher at Hermsdorf, just over one hundred kilometres south of Königsberg, a church whose living was in Dohna's gift. Ebel hesitated for a while, but eventually took up this post in 1807.

The young man's personal attachment to Schönherr and his teachings was well known and soon attracted the hostile scrutiny of the church authorities in the province. In 1809 the Church and School Deputation of the provincial government – the forerunner of what would later be the Provincial Consistory of East Prussia – demanded that Ebel answer official questions about his relationship with Schönherr: Were reports to the effect that he belonged among the adherents of Schönherr justified, and if they were, how did he believe it was possible to reconcile Schönherr's opinions with the official teachings of the evangelical-Lutheran Church? An investigation followed, but it merely confirmed that Ebel was beyond suspicion. Ebel himself stated in his own defence that he was a friend of Schönherr, not a disciple. And he challenged the Deputation to demonstrate that his teachings were irreconcilable with Holy Scripture. A personal reference supplied by the Church Superintendent in April 1810 stated that Ebel 'possessed true zeal for the good cause, was conscientious in all respects, including in his determination not to teach anything that does not belong among the duties of an evangelical-Lutheran clergyman'.

This might well have been the end of the matter. Ebel left his post at sleepy Hermsdorf in order to take up his teaching and preaching post at the Friedrichs-College in Königsberg. But the sceptics in the Deputation refused to give up. They continued to keep him under observation and persisted in their attacks. According to the reports of an unnamed informant, they claimed, Ebel was using his sermons and lectures to air convictions that carelessly invoked the devil as a real presence in the world, 'threatened the purity of the religious awareness among growing youth' and exhibited an attachment to separatist and sectarian principles irreconcilable with official doctrine.[1] Ebel was ordered to make a formal statement responding to these accusations and to clarify once again the nature of his current relationship with Schönherr.

Ebel took his time responding to this intervention, perhaps because he hoped that the Consistory would eventually persuade itself of the groundlessness of its own suspicions. But when it became clear that this was not going to happen, he broke his silence in a letter of 14 June 1814. This time the tone was more defiant. The first duty of a Protestant teacher, he wrote, was to honour 'the divinely revealed truth whose servant he is called to be', even if he faced the threat of persecution for doing so. His teaching method might be alien to the progressive 'spirit of the time', but it was entirely reconcilable with biblical truth. As for the devil, Luther was quite clear about his existence, wasn't that good enough for the gentlemen of the Deputation? Finally, the claim that Schönherr was a 'fanatical sectarian' was completely unfounded: 'He loves and seeks the truth with all of his heart. [. . .] Schönherr and I believe in the words of Jesus and his apostles (John 8; John 16; 1 Corinthians 2) and we strive in all humility to become and be righteous disciples of our saviour.'[2]

Appalled by the confrontational tone of this reply, the Deputation passed the entire file to the Department for Religion and Public Instruction in the Interior Ministry in Berlin, the organ that in 1817 would later become Carl von Altenstein's Kultusministerium. The Deputation requested that Ebel be removed from his clerical post and transferred to a school-teaching post. To the astonishment of Ebel's enemies, the Department did not just reject the request, but issued a sharp formal reproach to their colleagues in Königsberg. The complainants had failed to demonstrate that the teachings of Schönherr were irreconcilable with church doctrine – merely sending copies of his tracts was not sufficient because these contained only 'cosmogonic explanations which are intended to reinforce the authority of the Bible and which pose not the slightest threat to public morality'. The friendship between Ebel and Schönherr was completely irrelevant to the case because no public authority in the Kingdom of Prussia was authorized to 'interrogate a subordinate official about the company he keeps' unless these contacts evidently contravened 'the laws of morality and the state'. The ministry added that the fact that Ebel included the devil in his teachings could not be held against him, because it was not at all clear that this doctrine was not anchored in the Bible itself. The conclusion was a crushing defeat for the Ebel-bashers in the Königsberg Deputation:

The Difficult Ascent of Johann Ebel

It follows from the report and the supporting documents that the aforementioned Ebel has earned neither a transfer nor a suspension of his teaching offices in church and school. To impose either of these would thus be illogical and an act of violence, which would bring upon the ministry the suspicion of [precisely that] persecuting passion against which it believes it has good cause to warn the clerical and school deputation.[3]

The author of this ministerial decision, dated 28 August 1814, was none other than the theologian Friedrich Schleiermacher, then the holder of a theological chair at the newly founded University of Berlin and a senior functionary in the government department that in 1817 would evolve into the Kultusministerium. Schleiermacher was already famous as the author of *On Religion: Speeches to Its Cultured Despisers* (1799), in which he defended religion against the scepticism of people educated in the climate of the late Enlightenment. Schleiermacher was not an adherent of orthodoxy, whose doctrines he had personally largely abandoned. But nor was he an exponent of sceptical rationalism. He affirmed the fundamental value of what he called 'religious experience', which he viewed, in romantic fashion, as a constitutive attribute of human existence. In that turn-of-the-century world, when ideological positions appeared to be drifting further and further apart, Schleiermacher was not a polarizer but a reconciler and bridge-builder who hoped through an anthropological understanding of religion to mediate between faith and modern life. This orientation may have allowed him a certain sympathy with Ebel's aspiration to use Schönherr's teachings as a key to healing the rift between faith and science, even if it is unlikely that Schleiermacher was intellectually persuaded by the theosopher's confused cosmological speculations. On the other hand, he was certainly not impressed by the spirit of malice and narrow-minded harassment that appeared to animate Ebel's enemies in Königsberg. It is also possible that Schleiermacher knew of Ebel through his own connection with Friedrich Alexander, Count and Burgrave zu Dohna-Schlobitten, who had employed the young Schleiermacher and was among Ebel's early patrons. Schleiermacher was also, as the text of his judgement made clear, a defender of the freedom of religious teachers to accomplish their tasks by their own best lights, provided their instruction fell within the boundaries of the official doctrinal consensus.

The ministerial judgement of 28 August 1814 marked an inflection point. It was a signal that Ebel enjoyed official protection at the highest level, and that it would be unwise for his provincial enemies to persist in their efforts to disrupt his career. Ebel now entered a twenty-one-year period of relative peace and institutional security.[4] It was at this moment of growing confidence and expanding horizons that he counselled Ida von der Groeben. To her friends and family, the effect of Ebel's preaching and personal advice on Ida bordered on the miraculous. Ida returned to Königsberg society fully restored to the gaiety of her youthful self.

This was Ebel's definitive entry into Königsberg high society. He had always been drawn to the most elevated social milieus, but now he was treated like one of the family. The Auerswalds took him under their wing, so did the Kanitzes, the Münchows and other powerful clans. Society ladies flocked to his sermons. His future seemed assured: after all, until his retirement in 1824, Auerswald (Ida's father) was also, by virtue of his rank as President of the Province of Prussia, the chairman of the Consistorium, the supreme ecclesiastical council in the province, with responsibility for the appointment and

The Difficult Ascent of Johann Ebel

promotion of all clergymen. In 1816, Ebel was appointed archdeacon at the city's fashionable Altstadt Church.

Ebel was now at the apogee of his career, a celebrated figure in the city whose sermons were so popular that they emptied the churches of his rivals. His alliance with Pastor Diestel at the Haberberg Church created an axis that linked the aristocratic and mercantile elites of the city centre with the tradesmen of the Königsberg suburbs. Yet the success of these years also sowed the seeds of Ebel's later troubles. As we have seen, he was loathed by many of the clergymen of the city. Professional envy played a role here, but so did genuine distaste at the improvised theosophical doctrines he was rumoured to propagate alongside the official teachings of the Union Church. And these theological misgivings were soon joined by concern at the unconventionality of the relations supposedly cultivated among the women and men of his inner circle.

Altar of the Haberberg church, where Diestel preached. Photograph, 1897.

7.
The Ebelians

In a deposition requested by the authorities during the trial of Ebel, his friend and colleague Diestel tried to explain why people were drawn to him. He was a man of modesty and equanimity, always prepared to see the best in people, Diestel wrote. He was accessible to everyone without exception and all kinds of people, from the humblest to the most exalted, had a claim on his sympathy and help. There was a multifaceted quality and a suppleness to his nature that enabled him to situate himself imaginatively in the very particular situations his parishioners found themselves in; with the 'force of the love that was in him' he could be all things to all people, he could mediate the most diverse viewpoints, provided they contained something true. Diestel chose his words carefully: his intention was to push back against the notion that Ebel was or could be a sectarian leader. On the contrary he insisted, Ebel's nature was antipathetic to prejudices and partisan judgements: 'the trust he places without distinction in people, *because they are people*, tends by its nature to suspend divisive or isolating differences; worldly people and people of faith, rationalists and supernaturalists and [people of] the most diverse confessions find in the even-handedness of his personality an apt partner.'[1]

The cohesion of human associations is a fragile thing and the charisma of a single personality, however powerful, rarely suffices to sustain it over the longer term. In the case of the Ebelians, as they would later be known, the situation was complicated by the status of Schönherr as the venerated theosopher in the background whose philosophical 'key' Ebel and his friends had adopted as a means of vaccinating their faith against the objections of rationalists and sceptics.

Schönherr's lonely road from revelation to a fully blown theosophical theory, combined with the awe he seemed able to inspire in at least some of his followers, had left him with an exaggerated sense of his own powers. It became rare to see Schönherr without an entourage of disciples. And as his confidence grew, his behaviour became more erratic. The decision to build a self-propelling paddle-driven ship after a design that had come to him in a dream was one sign of increasing waywardness. Another was a tendency to see himself more and more as situated in a uniquely direct relationship with God. He came to believe that the redemption of the world would come simply from a general acknowledgement of the truth of his doctrine – a view that implied a relativization of the redemptive sacrifice of Christ. These were points of contrast with Ebel, who was inconspicuous and self-effacing in his manner and tended to elevate others rather than himself. Nor did he share Schönherr's exalted view of his revelation, instead Ebel saw it as a mere instrument for the strengthening of biblical faith, and he was worried by the way Schönherr de-emphasized Christ's redemptive achievement in order to foreground his own.

For some years, Ebel's conciliatory management of the relationships around him kept these tensions simmering below the surface. The break came when the physician Ludwig Wilhelm Sachs entered Ebel's circle. The pretext was Sachs's wish to take instruction in preparation for his conversion (and that of his wife and little boy) from Judaism to Christianity. Schönherr was excited by this news, because he believed that the physician, with his scientific training, would be excellently placed to understand, adopt, elaborate and propagate his own cosmological system.

...that Ebel instruct Sachs not just in Christianity but ...'s own theosophy. Ebel refused: he was a Christian ... a propagandist for Schönherr. Indignant, Schönherr ... for his own meeting with Sachs and used it to explain his views. Sachs – who had never lacked confidence in his own intellect – made no effort to hide his contempt for Schönherr's speculations. Enraged by the snub, Schönherr begged Ebel to suspend all further contact with Sachs until the doctor could be persuaded of the truth of his theosophical research. Ebel refused again and the older man's resentment grew.

As if this were not already enough, Schönherr proposed, in the spring and summer of 1819, a new redemptive instrument that could be used to support his cosmogonic theory, namely a kind of flagellation involving partial nakedness. This wasn't a completely gratuitous idea. It related to an eccentric interpretation of the passage at Galatians 5:24: 'And they that are Christ's have crucified the flesh with the affections and lusts'. When Ebel rejected this idea out of hand, Schönherr's sense of outrage deepened. He continued in vain to seek recruits for his flagellation scheme. After an open clash at a meeting of their circle, Ebel wrote him a letter in which he assured Schönherr of his love and friendship, but also refused to yield ground on their recent theological disagreements.

The problem was not just the divergence of viewpoints. It was also that Schönherr and Ebel were embarked on very different social trajectories. Whereas Schönherr was still offering his teachings on water and light to artisans, peddlers and wharfmen on the banks of the Pregel (though his audiences were shrinking as the style and content of his addresses became ever more outlandish), Ebel was addressing the cream of Königsberg high society. The adventurous days of the early post-war period were over and Schönherr was simply too unkempt and odd to follow Ebel into this new world. The separation, once initiated, was irreversible.

Ebel later tried to renew the contact, but Schönherr, embittered by what he saw as an unpardonable personal betrayal, refused ever again to receive the younger man. Ebel nevertheless continued whenever possible to provide his former mentor with financial help through a third party. However, the prophet of the Pregel was deserted by most of his followers. He died in poverty in 1826.

With Schönherr out of the way, Ebel's career flourished. His sermons were drawing huge crowds. The circle of enthusiasts around him steadily grew, as people who had worried about the eccentric teachings of Schönherr put aside their doubts. Women from the province's best families turned up in droves

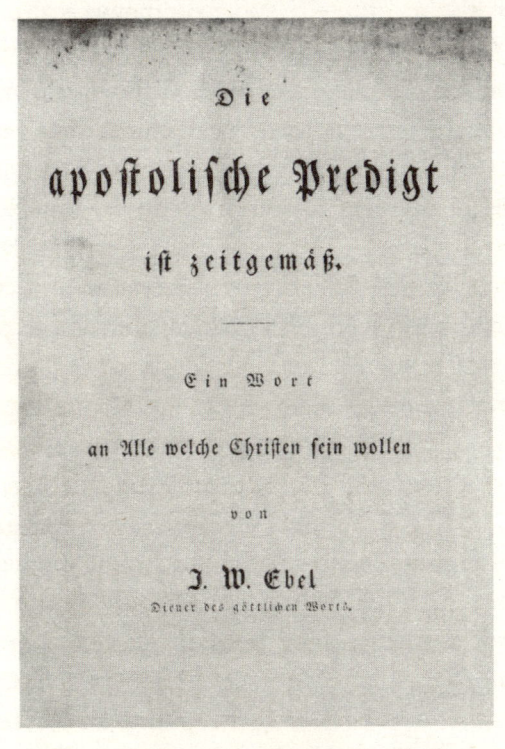

Title page to Johann Wilhelm Ebel, *Die Apostoliche Predigt ist zeitgemäß* (*The Preaching of the Apostles is Relevant Today*), 1835.

whenever Ebel preached. His sermons and occasional essays began to appear as books.

But there were also signs of future trouble. The administration remained hypersensitive to anything resembling religious separatism or zealotry. Throughout the 1820s, the Kultusministerium in Berlin circulated questionnaires to all the districts of the Prussian provinces. Every district government was required to fill in a form setting out an 'overview of the associations conducting extra-ecclesiastical religious rites or hours of devotion'. The questions to be answered included: 'Which associations exist and where?'; 'How large is the number of participants?'; 'Who leads the meetings?'; 'What do they [i.e. the meetings] consist of?'; and last but certainly not least: 'In what manner does their influence make itself felt on the lives of the participants and on the orientation of their spirits?' The replies from the District of Königsberg in 1822 revealed a range of local activities. In the parish of Altroßgarten there was a 'pious association' led by a gardener. There were '20 Pietists' in Schmelz. Far more numerous, especially in the inspectorate of Labiau to the east of Königsberg, were the 'Maldeniker', whose prayer and song meetings attracted hundreds of adherents. Their leaders were 'men of the lower class who believe themselves inspired', claimed the authority to interpret the scriptures and 'wander from one congregation to another'. Their meetings consisted of singing, praying, scriptural exegesis and religious discussions. The church superintendent charged with filing the report noted that these sectarians tended towards arrogance and exclusivism: they believed that they alone were 'clever, holy and deserving of salvation'. Those outside their circle were 'children of the devil'. It was rumoured that their supreme leader 'received his instructions from England', though the respondent added that this claim was as yet 'unverified'. The psychological effects were immediately apparent, since the adherents of this group were to be recognized by their 'wild glances, the rolling of their eyes and their distorted facial muscles'.[2] The answers of the district governments hint at the great variety of local religious activism, but they also bear eloquent witness to the fearfulness bordering on paranoia with which the Prussian authorities contemplated the religious energies at work in parts of the kingdom's society.

Of greater concern to Ebel and the people around him, because it was focused on the Province of East Prussia in particular, was a circular issued by the Ministry of Church Affairs in the autumn of 1825, urging the suppression of 'mystical, pietist and separatist' activities. The *Allgemeine Kirchenzeitung*, which published the circular on 21 January 1826, noted that the authorities were now keeping a watchful eye on 'perverse and pernicious trends' within the Protestant Church and were determined to take effective measures against them.[3] The new decree may not have been directed exclusively or even principally at Ebel – another prominent local target was the schoolteacher Peter Friedrich Theodor Kawerau, who was reported to be convening secret gatherings dedicated to the propagation of a supposedly better form of Christianity.[4] But the effect on Ebel's circle was chilling. During a meeting held at the house of Count Kanitz, a close friend and supporter of Ebel, early in 1826, the preacher urged two of his associates, the theologian Hermann Olshausen, an untenured professor at the University of Königsberg, and the theology student Friedrich Carl von Tippelskirch, to ask themselves whether they were prepared to remain in his circle, because being associated with Ebel was henceforth likely to hinder their professional advancement.

Ebel noted that things were likely to get tougher now that Hans von Auerswald had retired. His successor as President of the Province of Prussia, Theodor von Schön, was 'an antagonist of Christian faith and striving' who would like, if possible, to remove religion entirely from school education, on the grounds that it was merely a 'subjective attitude'. Schön disliked the elevated status of the churches within the state structure. He took them to be no more than 'free associations of individuals'. He insisted that religion was tolerable as a force in public life only when it was entirely subordinated to the imperatives of reason. As the President of the Province of Prussia, Schön, a man of progressive but not exactly liberal instincts with an exalted sense of his own power and importance, was the *ex officio* chair of the provincial church Consistory, the body tasked with overseeing the administration of the churches and appointments to clerical and theological posts. Ebel added that he would entirely understand if Olshausen and Tippelskirch thought it wiser under these circumstances to withdraw from his social circle. He assured them that they would remain his friends. According to Ida von der Groeben, who was present at this meeting, Olshausen listened intently to this advice and replied: 'Yes my dear Ebel, you are absolutely right, we need to think seriously about this.'[5] And sure enough, within two months, both men had

The Presidents of the provinces of the Kingdom of Prussia were not just senior administrators, but influential political bosses. Heinrich Theodor von Schön, 1834. Engraving by A. Teichel after a drawing by J. Wolff.

left the group. A year later, Olshausen received his reward in the form of a tenured professorship at the University of Königsberg.

But Olshausen went further than merely distancing himself from Ebel. He founded a secessionist anti-Ebelian circle, to which he tried to recruit Ebel's closest associates, and convened a regular gathering of preachers from Königsberg and the surrounding districts that soon evolved into a public conference at which Ebel and his followers were disparaged at every opportunity as proselytizing separatists and sectarians. On 4 March 1826, Ebel's forty-second birthday, Olshausen sent him a letter accusing him of arrogating to himself an inappropriate spiritual authority and creating a hierarchy whose effect was to suppress independent judgement. A battle of tracts and pamphlets began, in which Olshausen slugged it out with supporters of Ebel and especially Pastor Johann Georg Heinrich Diestel of the Haberberg Church. The bitter rivalry between Olshausen and the Ebelians belied the fact that both groups represented biblically oriented forms of Christianity that were opposed both to rationalism and to the religious indifference of a growing segment of the public. But the narrowness of the divergence did nothing to mute the bitterness of the conflict – it was a case study in the narcissism of small differences. Once the fight became more widely known, the secular-minded progressive East Prussian intelligentsia deemed both parties equally laughable and applied to both the derogatory term '*Mucker*' (pronounced to rhyme with 'booker'). The word was used in various German regions to denote an excessively and inauthentically pious person, but it also carried connotations of slyness, cunning, malice, hypocrisy and deceitfulness.[6] Among those who used it was Theodor von Schön, who wrote quizzically to Altenstein of the battle unfolding between 'two *Mucker*-societies' in his city.[7]

These quarrels among evangelical factions unfolded against the background of a deepening tension between evangelical and rationalist forms of Christian belief and practice. In an atmosphere of incipient culture war, the smallest provocations could flare into public altercations. In 1825, Friedrich Tholuck, the neo-pietist recruited by Altenstein to the Chair of Theology at Berlin, made disparaging remarks to a private gathering of English friends about the University of Halle, which he referred to as a 'place of unbelief'. In a process familiar from the controversies of our own time, the remark was passed on, picked up by an English newspaper, and also published by the orthodox and politically conservative *Evangelische Kirchenzeitung* in Berlin. There was a furious reaction from Halle. Tholuck issued a carefully worded public retraction: he was not as bad as people said he was and if they invited him to Halle, he would prove it.[8]

Among those whom Olshausen succeeded in recruiting from among the Ebelians after his own departure from the group were two figures who would play a key role in the scandal that followed. They were both men with a reputation for moral waywardness. Count Finck von Finckenstein had struggled – at least according to the testimony of his brother-in-law Count Kanitz, who knew him well – with 'earthly vice and vanity'. Having succumbed to 'passionate temptations', Finckenstein had 'fallen into a lower domain' but he had fought his way back up since 1822 and brought both his wife and his mother-in-law with him into Ebel's circle.[9] The physician Ludwig Wilhelm Sachs had come to Ebel seeking religious instruction, but it was widely known that he had battled with alcoholism and vagabond sexual urges. Both men, like other strugglers of this type, appear to have been drawn to Ebel as someone who could know of their weaknesses and even of their gross transgressions and yet remain committed to their forgiveness, improvement and redemption. But over the longer term, they both chafed at the moral reformism of the Ebel circle and the insistence that Christianity was not just a faith but a way of life that ought to reflect a strict moral code.

Finckenstein and Sachs both left the group in 1825. Finckenstein began almost immediately to echo the objections raised by Olshausen. Sachs had blended in well for a time, but when it became clear that his sexual misbehaviour had resumed, and doubts began to accumulate about academic malpractice and unprofessional behaviour with students, the people around Ebel pressed him to let the doctor go. Ebel resisted for a while, because he feared that abandonment would disarm Sachs against the worst promptings of his nature and plunge him back into his old ways. The issue was resolved in August 1825, when Count Kanitz sent Sachs a letter bristling with earnest reproaches and banning him from Ebel's society. This must have been an existential shock for Sachs, who owed several of his most valuable clients to the Ebel network – it was his proximity to Ebel that had persuaded a number of elite households to overcome their doubts and take him into their trust as family doctor.

Olshausen had earlier been among those who pressed Ebel to break with Sachs, but now he welcomed the doctor into his own counter-circle. Finckenstein's and Sachs's involvement in the fights that followed would set the tone of the scandal that engulfed Ebel and Diestel in 1835.

8.
Charge and Counter-Charge

By the end of 1834, Count Finck von Finckenstein's resentment of Ebel had reached boiling point. Pecuniary anxieties helped to deepen the animosity. The count had fallen out with his sister, Charlotte Henriette Karoline Elisabeth, Countess Finck von Finckenstein, over an inheritance. Finckenstein was personally of the view that only sons should inherit family property; sisters ought to depend on the generosity of their brothers. He proposed to her that she forego the interest payable on her portion of the paternal inheritance, which consisted of a share in the family estate on which her brother lived. She did not surrender her claim, but she agreed for the time being to renounce the greater part of the interest payments owing on her portion. The issue became entangled with the religious conflicts around Ebel because whereas Finckenstein had left Ebel's circle in 1826, Charlotte remained loyal. Even so, she continued to honour the financial arrangement she had agreed with her brother.

The situation changed in 1830, when Charlotte's husband, the Ebel loyalist Count Kanitz, was obliged on account of his health to make a series of expensive journeys to spas for which his own income as a state functionary was not sufficient. Charlotte now asked her brother to begin paying her half of the interest owing on her portion. Finckenstein was furious. After a rancorous exchange, he agreed to pay her in full each year, but further contacts were handled with such anger and rudeness on his part that Charlotte tired of the arrangement between them and called in her capital – meaning the full value of her portion and the hitherto unpaid interest. The funds were to be delivered in three instalments, payable over three years. Finckenstein was delirious with rage. He focused his ire on Ebel, whom he wrongly believed to have instigated Charlotte's claim behind the scenes.

Towards the end of 1834, Finckenstein learned that a female cousin was in the process of joining the Ebel circle and warned her against having anything to do with them, hinting at horrific threats to her virtue and health. The cousin told her sister, Zelina von Mirbach, a woman with Ebelian sympathies, who wrote to Finckenstein demanding an explanation. His reply kicked off the chain of events that would become known as the 'Königsberg religious trial'.

In his letter of reply to Zelina, Finckenstein explained that Ebel taught his followers a load of nonsense about water balls and fire balls. This delusion was wrapped in pretty and high-sounding words and went by the name 'Knowledge of the two Primordial Beings'. The true observation on which it was based was simply the fact that there is a male and a female version of every created being. Yet the untenability of the claim about water balls and fire balls was obvious as soon as it was expressed in plain and simple words. The practical implication of the teaching, Finckenstein went on, was that believers must live in consciousness of the doctrine of the two 'original beings' and thus must strive to purify the relations between the two sexes. How should one do this? According to Finckenstein, the answer offered by Ebel was that since everything was 'pure and holy' among those who had already sanctified themselves by accepting the Schönherr doctrine, the elect would be obliged to 'make ever more room for the low and – as I would call it – bestial sexual drive'. The key thing was 'always and in every moment to retain mastery over it'. In his pursuit of this objective, Finckenstein claimed in his letter, Ebel had permitted himself some hair-raising perversities. He had not merely recommended an immoral encounter with a woman as a means of sanctification; much worse, 'he urged me by means of hints on a number of occasions to do this *in his presence*, which I didn't do, praise be to God!'[1]

The dangers posed by such unbridled debauchery could scarcely be overstated, Finckenstein continued in the letter. He had 'heard' that there had been deaths as a consequence of the libertine excesses within Ebel's circle. 'This is Satan's work on these poor people, this is the rotten fruit, these are the dangers that threaten all girls who join the Ebel group. And this is why only women or male hermaphrodites are interested in joining it.' The focus was mainly on Ebel, but Diestel made a cameo appearance in the context of a discussion about whether or not Ebel's followers actually believed in all this primordial claptrap: 'Whether Diestel, who came to the circle later, is a hypocrite or not, I cannot say.'[2]

These were strong accusations, and it is not surprising that Zelina decided to show Finckenstein's letter to her friend Pastor Diestel. She may have been hoping that he would put her own doubts to rest. Or perhaps she simply thought that he should be aware of the calumnies circulating against him and his mentor and close friend Johann Ebel. Whichever it was, the effect was explosive. Ebel was a mild-mannered, fey man, self-effacing and conciliatory. Diestel was not any of these things. He was headstrong, passionate, intensely protective of his friend Ebel and very easily angered. In a letter to Finckenstein running to twenty-nine large folios, Diestel verbally savaged the count in words snarled through gritted teeth, addressing him with the eye-to-eye menace of the intimate *Du*:

> I will not tolerate it, dear Finck; I will not let my person, I will not let the name I have acquired as a Christian pastor be denigrated. The words you wrote, the disgraceful impression you tried to make, I will erase them in those in whom the last traces of truth and right have not been erased, for my sake, for God's sake and the sake of the people by whom and for whom I was entrusted with this office. I have decided, dear Finck, to put an end to your machinations and I will lame your slandering tongue . . .[3]

There followed an obsessive retracing of remembered infamies, bristling with scare quotes and incantatory repetitions. If you had been Diestel's friend and he asked you to take a look at a draft before he popped the letter into the post, you would probably have urged him to cut it down to a page or two, trim the invective and focus on a few key points. But there was no stopping Diestel in his indignant rage – he was going to 'annihilate' the 'miserable lying brat' Finckenstein; he was going to 'crush' him underfoot.

It was the calumnies against Ebel and the Ebelians that infuriated Diestel most: 'such disgraceful libels can only have been fabricated in the latrine of a disgraceful world view and can only have flowed over disgraceful lips . . .'. With the 'filth' of his own unclean mind, Finckenstein had dared to besmirch others purer and more chaste than he. Who could fault Ebel, Diestel asked, for practising and teaching a form of Christianity that aspired to 'sanctify every domain of human life *without exception*, to sanctify and ennoble social and domestic relationships, to sanctify and ennoble not just churches but also houses, not just meeting halls but also bedrooms, and by no means with the intention of making the former into conventicle chambers and the latter into brothels'? And why on earth should the bedroom of a married couple fall outside the remit of a Christian pastor? After all, the Gospels themselves included injunctions in relation to correct conduct within marriage (Hebrews 13:4 and 1 Peter 3:7). Only a contaminated spirit could possibly find perversity in this.[4]

With Diestel's incendiary missive, the animosities seething within a network of people who knew each other well became enmeshed with the administrative and legal machinery of the province and with the public life of the city of Königsberg. Finck von Finckenstein handed the correspondence over to the Criminal Court, which immediately launched an investigation against Diestel. The Provincial Consistory of East Prussia now called upon Finckenstein to substantiate his charges against the Ebelians.

9.
Building a Case

In handling the issues raised by the investigation into Ebel and Diestel, the Consistory – the administrative organ of the Union Church in the Prussian provinces – had to keep in mind a double purpose. On the one hand, it was important that the Consistory have the means to act against a clergyman who had breached professional discipline. On the other, it needed to be in a position to support church employees who were subjected to unfounded accusations. In short, the Consistory had to strike a balance between disciplinary vigilance and the duty of care, and it was expected to do so from the standpoint of neutrality and strict regard for fair process. This last point is important, because in 1814, as we have seen, the Church and School Deputation of the Königsberg government, the administrative predecessor of the Consistory, had already been cautioned by the authorities in Berlin for pursuing Ebel in a spirit of 'persecuting passion' and harassing him with coercive and 'illogical' measures.

By the mid-1830s, when the scandal around Ebel blew up, there was little reason to suppose that the Consistory would adopt a supportive view of its beleaguered employee. From 1824, when he became President of the Province of Prussia, Theodor von Schön was also the *ex officio* chairman of the Consistory. Schön was one of the most gifted officials in the kingdom of Prussia. As a young man he had been among the reformers who refashioned the kingdom's economy and administration. From 1809, he held a series of increasingly senior administrative posts. In 1816, Frederick William III appointed him to the Presidency of West Prussia, with an official residence in the city of Danzig. In 1824, with the departure from office of Ida's father Hans Jakob von Auerswald, West Prussia and East Prussia were formed into one entity and Schön was appointed President of the new amalgamated province, with his headquarters in the royal castle in Königsberg.

No one more completely embodied the tone and outlook of the Königsberg enlightenment than this 'radical Kantian', as Karl Rosenkranz called his friend Theodor von Schön. Schön was a tireless reformer whose interests ran from artificial fertilizers and the extraction of beet sugar to farming machines, sheep husbandry and the construction of highways. His zest for improvement was coupled with high ambition and self-confidence. In 1817, when he was still Oberpräsident of West Prussia in Danzig, he wrote a memorandum with the title: 'What Can an Oberpräsident be?' It was signed by all of the Oberpräsidenten of the Prussian provinces. In it, they demanded a position as 'independent men' with direct access to the king, and without the ministers getting in between.[1] The surviving letters and diaries reveal that Schön was an arrogant personality, quick to criticize and attack his contemporaries.[2] Ida von der Groeben, a critical but well-informed observer of her brother-in-law, described him as a man indifferent to religion and consumed by vanity and political ambition. The soirées he presided over at his residence in Königsberg were famous for their irreverent and 'unspiritual' (*geistlos*) tone. Schön teased her at every opportunity about her piety and provoked her with calumnies against Ebel. In 1829, when the Empress of Russia, who happened to be Princess Charlotte, daughter of the Prussian king, passed through Königsberg, she asked after Ida, whom she remembered as a childhood friend. Theodor von Schön replied: 'She doesn't get to see anyone; she belongs to a sect.'[3]

Schön was also involved in the campaign to demolish the Old City Church on the grounds that structural weaknesses rendered the building unfit for purpose. One of his first acts as President of the Province of Prussia was an order despatched from Marienburg – before he had even arrived in the city to take up his post! – stipulating that the church should be torn down. Ebel was ordered to move into a temporary alternative venue, to which his congregation happily followed him. But members of the Old City parish succeeded in getting an inspector from Berlin to issue the church with a good bill of health, and other weighty figures spoke up for its preservation. The battle for the church dragged on into the 1830s. In 1834 the Government Building Inspector, a close ally of Schön, argued that the square on which the church stood could no longer carry its weight. Ebel managed to have another square selected as suitable for a replacement building, but Schön made it clear that he intended not just to shut down the church, but to suppress the parish altogether and reassign its resources to neighbouring congregations. On Ebel's behalf, Count Kanitz succeeded in securing the support of the king, who was opposed to Schön's campaign to dissolve the Old City parish.[4]

These manoeuvres angered Schön, and he must have been in a receptive mood at the beginning of 1834, when Finckenstein sought him out at a meeting of the Danzig Provincial Diet. Finckenstein was hoping to get Schön to support him in securing a loan to cover the cost of paying off his sister's inheritance claim, but he also told Schön that the deterioration in Finckenstein's relationship with his sister was the direct result of Ebel's religious fanaticism, since it arose from the fact that she had remained loyal to the clergyman and his 'sect', whereas he had not. Finckenstein probably also hinted at the sexual improprieties that were supposedly proliferating among Ebel's followers.

As the *ex officio* chairman of the East Prussian Consistory, Schön entrusted the leadership of the investigation that followed Finckenstein's denunciation to the theologian, preacher and Consistorial Councillor Ludwig August Kähler. However, Kähler was not an impartial bystander. This intelligent, eloquent man had once been a rationalist of the late eighteenth-century type, but by the 1810s and 1820s, like not a few of his contemporaries, he had traced a path towards a hybrid religiosity that combined an esteem for reason with a respect for mystery and sentiment – 'for a Christian, feeling and reason are as inseparable as freedom of action and freedom of thought; they inform, illuminate and determine each other.'[5] This makes him sound like a close neighbour of Ebel and Diestel, who were both hopeful bridge-builders between reason and faith. But Kähler had no time for what he saw as Ebel's cliquish and sectarian mysticism. He attacked Ebel in various sermons and the two-volume treatise he published in the form of a dialogue in 1823 and 1824 (under the unwieldy title: *Philagathos. Insinuations about the Kingdom of Goodness. An Explanation of Christian-Religious Truth for Friends of the Same*) was widely read in Königsberg as a lightly disguised attack on Ebel and his followers. At one point in this text, Kähler describes a young woman's initiation into a community of 'saints' who welcome her with a shower of passionate kisses. Only when she is approached by a young man known to be a sexual profligate does she flee the scene and seek the counsel of her parents. In 1828, Kähler had urged his colleagues on the Consistory to appoint an adjunct to the preacher's post at the Old City Church, who could be used to keep Ebel under surveillance and undermine his independence. The Consistory, as the senior provincial disciplining authority of the Church, supported this proposal, but the city government did not, and nothing came of it.[6]

From the very beginning, the Consistory went out of its way to build a case against Ebel and Diestel. Among those whom Kähler invited to make a deposition to the Consistory was Dr Ludwig Wilhelm Sachs, who had left Ebel's circle under a cloud and was known to be a hostile witness. On the basis of depositions by Finckenstein and Sachs, Kähler composed an official statement on behalf of the Consistory. The statement itself is no longer extant – the bulk of the East Prussian consistorial archive was destroyed at the end of the Second World War and only fragments made it to the GDR State Archives at Merseburg and later to the Geheimes Staatsarchiv in Berlin. But according to the summary of Count Kanitz, who read this document in the spring of 1836, it affirmed that Ebel and Diestel had propagated a 'dangerous doctrine' irreconcilable with the official teachings of the Church, and whose 'corrupting effects' had made themselves felt in the 'immoral behaviour' of those who preached and adopted their doctrine.

In following this course, Kähler departed from standard procedure. By calling witnesses to testify against Ebel, the Consistory acted as an investigative body, when its official task was simply to monitor the progress of the case between Finckenstein and Diestel. Sachs did not make his deposition in the official premises of the Consistory, as was standard procedure, but in the private apartments of Dr Kähler himself. Had Kähler intended to produce an expert opinion (*Gutachten*) worthy of the name, he ought to have conducted an independent investigation aimed at ascertaining what the 'Schönherr–Ebel doctrine' actually was, whether it was in fact propagated systematically by Ebel or Diestel, whether it indeed conflicted with the official teachings of the Church, and whether it could truly be said to have had 'corrupting' effects. Instead, Kähler's report merely paraphrased the accusations of persons known to be hostile to Ebel and his associates.[7] No thought was given to the Church's duty of care towards the clergymen in its employ, nor to shielding them from the impact of as yet unproven allegations. The Consistory had joined the prosecution.

10.
The Trial Begins

From the outset, the odds were stacked against Ebel, Diestel and their supporters. After Kähler had penned his official statement, the Consistory invited Ebel to attend for an interview on 2 October 1835. Three days before the interview, he asked to be shown the prosecution documents, so that he might know who was accusing him and read the substance of their accusations. When this request was refused, he appeared at the appointed time, but declared that he would not issue a statement of any kind until his earlier request had been granted. Although no actual evidence had as yet been gathered in support of the prosecution, the Consistory took the highly significant step of suspending Ebel from office – a step it had, strictly speaking, no right or reason to take. Under the regulations in force at the time, the Consistory was obliged to ask the Ministry of Church Affairs before taking such a step, but it did not do so. Reporting on the interview, Kähler noted that Ebel took the news of his suspension 'calmly and cheerfully'.[1]

Three weeks later, in another major departure from recommended practice, Kähler published an anonymous article in the *Allgemeine Kirchenzeitung* outlining the nature of the charges against the accused and offering two justifications for the decision to suspend Ebel. The first was respect for 'public opinion' (*die allgemeine Stimme*), given that 'the public is waiting impatiently and irritably, and in a spirit overwhelmingly hostile to

Ebel and his friends, for a decisive intervention, and sees Ebel's suspension from office as such'. And the other reason was that Ebel had 'refused to make a statement and took measures that were designed to delay the investigation as much as possible'.[2] Both of these claims were specious. It was Kähler and his allies in the city's upper strata who favoured action against Ebel and Diestel, not popular opinion in the city. And it was disingenuous to suggest that Ebel's request to see an official transcript of the charges against him was merely a delaying tactic.

The Consistory adopted a similarly prejudicial procedure in respect of Diestel. First, they told him to explain 'to what extent he [agreed] with the principles of which Ebel [had] been accused of advocating.' He replied on 15 October 1835 that he was in agreement with his colleague and friend Ebel on all important dogmatic and moral points. In response, the Consistory ordered him to promise that he would not make any direct or indirect reference to the issues in contention in his sermons or other official utterances. When Diestel refused to make this undertaking, he, too, was placed under investigation. Statements were solicited from District Commissioner (*Landrat*) Adolf von Hake of Dargau and the city councillor Moisiszig. Here again, the procedure adopted was disadvantageous to the accused. Commissioner von Hake had once been an admirer and friend of Ebel and a member of his close circle, but he had left under a cloud at the same time as Finckenstein. Moisiszig was an unsuitable informant, because he was at this time the accountant on Finckenstein's estate and thus unlikely to be able to provide unbiased testimony. Nevertheless, their statements sufficed to have Diestel suspended from office on 9 December 1835. Five days later, a criminal investigation was opened against him.

Once the trial got under way, the two men engaged as trial

advocate for the defence a court clerk who had only recently begun to practise in Königsberg. Ludwig Crelinger was a highly intelligent man of around forty who had been forced to go into the law by the sudden evaporation of his father's substantial fortune. Fanny Lewald, in whose house he was a lodger, described him as 'spirited, witty, lively and sensual, and always enthused by what was beautiful and great'. He was new to Königsberg and the already notorious trial of Ebel and Diestel promised him a fast track to local renown and well-heeled clients. Crelinger, though an unlikely temperamental match for the two accused clergymen, proved an excellent choice. In a long sequence of written objections, he poked holes in witness testimony and identified numerous breaches of good procedure, and denounced them in clear, forensic language. The court, he argued, had failed to test the case built up by the Consistory against the standard criteria for a prosecution. The Consistory had applied on the grounds of 'suspicion of the establishment of a sect whose doctrines lead to vice', but the court had done nothing to establish whether such a crime had in fact been committed. Had the application been appraised in the light of the documents, it would have become clear that the reference to an illegal sect was an interpolation by Kähler and did not match with the protocols of the depositions by Finckenstein and Sachs, neither of whom referred to a sect. The accusers had not provided proper depositions before the court, as required by the Prussian General Law Code, and no one had bothered to scrutinize the relationships between the accusers, the prosecution witnesses and the accused, or among the accusers and their witnesses. The judges had failed in most instances to distinguish between hearsay and eyewitness testimony, meaning that several of the key witnesses were allowed to testify to events and actions they had not personally witnessed. The efforts of the defence to challenge the alleged evidence of the witnesses on these grounds had been in vain. And no effort had been made (as required by §§ 108 and 110 of the Prussian Criminal Code) to ensure that the good names of the accused be protected until their possible conviction.³

Ebel's supporters did not remain inactive. Count Kanitz composed a long statement summarizing the case and insisting on Ebel's and Diestel's complete innocence, but the Consistory refused to add this document to the official file. On 12 October 1835, Kanitz wrote to Minister Altenstein complaining of how the investigation had been handled. Dr Ebel's reputation was 'too deeply based among the better part of our contemporaries' to allow such suspicions to resonate. On all sides, and not only among the numerous congregation of the Old City and the Haberberg churches but among many other inhabitants of the city, the 'hasty steps' of the authorities against Ebel were seen as an act of violence and administrative caprice. This was a significant observation because it challenged the claim that the aroused state of the public had forced the Consistory, and its chairman, President Theodor von Schön, to act swiftly against the 'sectaries'.

Ida von der Groeben also wrote to Altenstein because, like Kanitz, she distrusted the authorities in the province. In a cover letter of 18 October 1835, she reminded Altenstein of his friendship with her father, Hans Jakob von Auerswald, former President of the Province of Prussia, and of her own warm youthful memories of the minister during the years after 1806–7, when Altenstein was one of the cohort of reformers who had gathered in Königsberg to restructure the Prussian state and Ida was the teenage daughter of a distinguished functionary. There followed a long and convoluted text, bearing the title, 'Request to be heard', in which the countess set out her view of the background to the current investigation.

For many years, she wrote, Count Finck had been 'creeping about the Province', circulating secret calumnies against Archdeacon Ebel, the preacher Diestel and other respectable persons. Ebel had only come under suspicion because he stood for an ethically rigorous Christianity that was an affront to the troubled consciences of those unable to follow his advice. Instead of handling the accusations against the two clergymen in an impartial way, she argued, the Consistory had placed itself on the side of the slanderers. Contrary to the claims broadcast in the press, Ida wrote, Ebel had always spoken out against those who embraced sectarian activity, which he saw as symptoms of 'inertia of the spirit', 'an affection for mystical and intoxicating emotions', and 'antipathy towards practical Christianity'. He had always opposed sectarianism in his sermons and essays, life and behaviour. As for Ebel's personal philosophical convictions, Ida insisted that Ebel had never propagated these; on the contrary he had always been aware of the conditionality (*Bedinglichkeit*) of philosophical research and was at pains to warn against idle indulgence in speculation, cosmological or otherwise – it was precisely this that had sown discord between him and his friend Schönherr. On the other hand, he had indeed taught that the theory of the primordial beings was a key by means of which the truth contained in the old teachings of the Church could at last be made plausible. As such, he argued, it was an excellent antidote to the general disbelief in biblical truth that could be found even in the ranks of the ecclesiastical administration of this city:

> He worked hand to counter the confusion to which people are prey, deploying against it his sober understanding and

A Scandal in Königsberg

explained the implacable strictness of the moral law revealed in the divine commandments, stripped of the obfuscation and uncertainty [. . .], in a nakedness that is terrifying for those who have not the stomach for it. This is what made his teachings so hateful to many.[4]

The text – which ran to ten large folios – closed with an entreaty: the state must intervene to stop the Consistory treating virtuous churchmen as if they were a band of robbers, and it must summon the slanderers themselves to justice. Among the recipients of further letters from Ida was Crown Prince Frederick William, the future Frederick William IV, a man of evangelical religious sympathies, who wrote to Altenstein on 28 October 1835 saying that he had no intention of getting directly involved in this controversy but that he would like to be kept informed of the progress of the 'sectarian story' in Königsberg.[5]

Frederick William in 1835, when he was still Crown Prince of Prussia. Engraving by Auguste Hüssener after Franz Krüger.

II.
Diestel Testifies

Whereas Ebel had refused to answer the questions of the Consistory until he was shown the charge sheet, Diestel was more forthcoming and provided his inquisitors with long and nuanced answers during his questioning on 15 and 16 October 1835. Asked whether he acknowledged the doctrine of 'two primordial beings' referred to by Schönherr as a 'foundational doctrine' (*Grundsatz*) and whether he adhered to a system based upon it, he replied, 'I must answer with no', and added, 'In making this answer, I proceed from the view that I could only acknowledge this teaching as one of my axiomatic principles if I already understood thoroughly and precisely its context and its consequences.'[1]

This answer made sense against the background of Diestel's relationship with Schönherr. Diestel had met the theosopher already in 1805: 'Early on the very first evening when I visited him, Schönherr informed me of the basic principles of his system.' This rings true: Schönherr was not one to wait until the second evening to get started on the serious stuff. But at that time, his expositions left Diestel 'uncertain and undecided'. In retrospect it was clear that the teachings of Schönherr were less important to Diestel than the 'lively religious outlook and the pure ethical commitment' that he recognized as 'fundamental attributes of [the theosopher's] character'. Shortly afterwards, Diestel left the province. When he returned in 1809, there was no renewal of the contact. Only in 1822, after four years of close friendship with Ebel, did Diestel once again take an interest in Schönherr, not because he hoped to adopt his 'system', but rather because he had come to understand that Ebel did not assign to Schönherr's insights an absolute value (as Schönherr himself did), but only a relative one, focused on the salutary and healing effect they could have on the life of individuals. Whereas Schönherr and his increasingly few disciples believed that salvation would follow simply from embracing his vision, Ebel's was a selective adaptation – he only endorsed the theosopher's teachings to the extent that they promoted 'the sole and highest purpose of life', namely the gathering of the faithful to God.[2]

Diestel acknowledged in his testimony before the Consistory that he believed the doctrine of the two primordial beings was confirmed in scripture, but he added that he was as yet in no position to demonstrate that this was the case in relation to 'all of its aspects'. In the written statement he supplied to the Consistory on the first day of his interrogation, he even wrote: 'I am neither a friend nor an admirer of the beard that Schönherr wore, and even less of the ship that he had built, and nor is Preacher Ebel.'[3]

This was, then, at best a rather partial and ambivalent statement of adherence to the teaching of Schönherr. Yet the summary of the deposition composed by the Consistory stated that Diestel acknowledged he believed 'in the existence of two primordial beings', that he found 'this belief to be confirmed by passages in holy scripture', that he claimed to be on the path towards using these insights to 'solve all the problems of philosophy', and they inferred from this that he was 'heading in an extremely dangerous direction, given his activity as a pastor'.[4]

Much of the interrogation focused on allegations to the

effect that Ebel and Diestel had encouraged sexually licentious behaviour among their followers. Was it true that the Ebelians had been encouraged to use sexual intimacy, and specifically the 'unnatural over-arousal of the body' as a means of 'purification'? Diestel replied with a vehement denial. He was repelled by the idea of the concerted pursuit of sexual pleasure for its own sake. Asked whether he had ever dispensed advice on sexual matters, he replied: 'Yes, both Dr Ebel and I gave advice: for example, that consciousness and purity of attitude [*Reinheit der Gesinnung*] must prevail, and that intimacy must not be darkened by animalistic drives and lusts [. . .]. But we never delivered our views in the form of a general instruction, and nor did we deduce from them any particular ritual [*Ritus*].' Rather, the two men had offered 'pieces of advice calibrated to the differing individuality [of the persons under our pastoral care] for the reining in of unconscious drives and for bending these to the mastery of consciousness'. It was thus false to claim that Ebel or Diestel had ever placed the purification of the sexual relationship between spouses at the centre of some larger programme of 'sanctification' (an important point because this claim would recur in many of the press commentaries on the case). Nor had Diestel or Ebel ever urged their friends or parishioners to make special confessions to each other, sexual or otherwise. On the other hand, they had certainly commended the 'open acknowledgement of sin', though only in cases where they 'believed it was suitable in light of the moral standing of the relevant individual'.

Was it true, the consistorial councillors asked on the second day, that the two clergymen had commended 'the contemplation of nakedness' (*der Anblick des Nackten*) to their parishioners in the context of discussions of sexual relations? Yes, Diestel replied, Dr Ebel urged the married men who took him into their confidence with concerns about the quality or moral status of their conjugal relations, not to make love to their wives with the lamp extinguished, but rather in the light, because, as Ebel put it: 'the contemplation of nakedness could help to free the fantasy from its images and transform blind lust into conscious affection for the spouse'. Taken out of context, of course, Ebel's phrase *'der Anblick des Nackten'* (the contemplation of nakedness) could be made to sound voyeuristic or even pornographic. The claim made in the press that Ebel and Diestel had offered this and other similar advice to unmarried persons, thereby inciting them to 'immorality', was never substantiated. Both men strenuously denied it. Diestel also denied that either of the two men had ever encouraged the stimulation of sexual urges outside the context of procreative coupling between spouses. Diestel insisted that he abhorred, and had never endorsed, the idea of 'artificially over-exciting the body'.[5]

In his written statement to the Consistory, Diestel explained that both he and Ebel shared the firm conviction that there were two kinds of shame. The first – an instinctive revulsion in the face of perversity and licentiousness – was an essential social check on vice. The second – the private shame that a wife or husband might feel when she or he was naked before the eyes of the partner – was a 'false' or 'superficial' shame that ought to have no place in the intimate lives of loving spouses who strove to live in conformity with the teaching of Christ. We find a very similar characterization of Ebel's thinking on shame in the memoirs of Eduard von Hahnenfeld, a supporter, who recalled learning from him that the feeling of shame was 'a precious good worthy of preservation, as the witness of the Holy Spirit within us, to the fact that we are sinful and have fallen from our calling'. But at the same time, Ebel had 'tried anew to commend the ennoblement and hallow of marriage, just as Luther had done'. And like Luther before him, Ebel was now being 'slandered and persecuted' by the 'refined indecency of our time' for the purity of his motives.[6]

A highly distorted version of this teaching circulated in the press in the form of the rumour that Ebel and Diestel believed sin to be impossible in the intimate relations between 'sanctified ones', even if they were not married. In reality, neither man had ever taught that the purification of sexual relations was the 'key to sanctification' for all individuals or that it should take place outside marriage.

It is interesting to note that these injunctions on the conduct of intimate life did not emerge as abstract doctrinal positions, but always in the context of specific conversations between pastors and their parishioners. The accusations by Moisiszig and von Hake were both based on claims about 'instructions' supposedly issued by Ebel and Diestel in the context of pastoral contacts. When he was asked whether he had ever provided City Councillor Moisiszig with 'instruction about sexual relations', Diestel replied that although his relationship with the councillor had once been very close, they had had no contact for several years (Moisiszig had left the circle at the same time as his employer Finckenstein). But Diestel did remember, around 1826, an occasion on which he had spoken with Moisiszig. 'This occurred at his request and after he had informed me what had happened in this respect within his own marital relationship. What I told him I don't know. But I am convinced that he was not astonished by it, as he claims he was in his statement . . .' Diestel was also asked whether he had provided District Commissioner von Hake with instructions on how he should conduct himself in his marriage. 'I do remember however, that he spoke to me and that I spoke to him about experiences acquired in marriage. That was all there was to it since he did not ask me for my advice.'⁷

Count Finck von Finckenstein, too, parlayed claims about the content of private conversations with the accused into his public denunciations. He claimed, as we have seen, that Ebel had expressed to him the desire to be present while he was making love with his wife. Asked to comment on this allegation, Diestel produced an earlier letter from Finckenstein's wife Wilhelmine (originally addressed to her sisters, but later passed to Diestel), in which she had reported that it was her husband (i.e. Finckenstein himself) who had proposed this as a means of helping him to make love to her: 'it could help me most, if I imagine that a third person, who I know has sanctified himself in the Lord, were present as well and I can very easily think of such a person, before whose eyes we could make love'.⁸

Why Finckenstein felt that he would find it easier to engage in sexual intercourse with his wife if Ebel were standing to one side looking on is anyone's guess. What these allegations above all revealed, Diestel suggested in his own deposition to the Consistory, was the vulnerability of the clergyman charged with pastoral responsibility for stressed or endangered marriages. When marriages broke apart, releasing formerly private resentments, the pastor who had attempted to guide both partners could find himself in an exceptionally exposed position.⁹ We actually know very little about this aspect of the historical role of the pastor, who was not simply a teacher and celebrant, but also – *avant la lettre* – a marriage councillor and therapist. In an article exploring the visceral hatred of nineteenth-century (male) French republicans for the Catholic clergy, the historian Ralph Gibson observed that the role of the priest as the first (and often only) source of counsel and comfort for women in unhappy marriages was a source of profound resentment among republican male heads of household.[10] Exactly what advice Ebel and Diestel dispensed to parishioners in a wide range of personal predicaments we will never know, but it is striking that so many male contemporaries saw them as disruptors of family harmony and alienators of women from their husbands. It may also be that their efforts to rein in the sexual urge, to subordinate it to love and reason, appealed to the women of their circle more than to the men. Ebel conceded in a letter to the Ministry of Church Affairs that he had been 'libelled for years by people who formerly enjoyed my pastoral care', and he added that this was the consequence of the rigour with which he had monitored the morality of the individuals who submitted to his supervision.[11] Although many men can be heard in the files complaining of and attacking the two clergymen, I have yet to find a single female complainant.

12.
A Media Sensation

The public excitement generated by these allegations was remarkable. King Frederick William III wrote to Altenstein expressing his indignation at the fact that such a sensitive matter was being so widely discussed in the newspapers.[1] The populace, Theodor von Schön reported, was 'worked up' by the affair. Students descended on the services attended by Ebelians, rowdily demanding 'seraphic kisses' from the ladies as they left church. Lampoons appeared on street corners.[2] The press hounded Ebel unmercifully, and not just in Königsberg.[3] The more anodyne accounts confined themselves to ridiculing the theological preoccupations of the *'Mucker'* – the term is widely used in coverage of the scandal. A rather arch commentary from the *Staats- und Gelehrten-Zeitung des Hamburgischen Correspondenten* of 1 April 1836 noted that although the 'trial of the Königsberg *Mucker*' was being held in secret in order to avoid public offence, it was already possible, on the basis of what was already known, to say that the case was likely to be as rich in lessons for psychology as for the history of doctrine. The rest of the article depicted the ideas of the accused as a laughable confection of 'mysteriosophical' speculations reminiscent of the gnostics, Manicheans, Saturnians and Basilideans of olden times.[4] Refracted through the pages of printed commentary, the inner life of the Ebel–Diestel 'sect' became a kind of virtual reality, quite uncoupled from verifiable observations. Suggestive hints and vague intuitions could be as important as allegations of specific outrages. 'I was already at this time getting disquieting impressions of something hidden in the interior of the circle which had gathered around the above-named clergyman,' wrote Consistorial Councillor Kähler, who had left the group in 1823, in an anonymous piece for the *Evangelische Kirchenzeitung* on 9 March 1836. 'Punishable facts were unknown to me when I separated myself [from the Ebel group],' wrote Kähler. 'Only after leaving did I learn of such things through other people.'[5]

Other reports were more explicit. 'The aberrations in religion, the immoralities, the activities insulting to Christian faith [perpetrated by the Ebelians] are such that a chaste pen cannot describe them', frothed an article in the Leipzig newspaper *Unser Planet*. The author went on to describe in exquisite detail one of the rites supposedly conducted within the circle. A certain gentleman had hoped to ascend from the lower to the higher 'level' [*Grad*] of the 'sect'. He was summoned into Ebel's presence:

> ... and received the instruction to pray kneeling in an antechamber, in order to prepare himself for this important step. After he had kneeled and prayed for some time, the door of a dimly lit adjoining room opened. In the dull glow of a lamp, the Leader of the sect could be seen on a sofa with a beautiful young girl from one of the finest families of the city on his lap. He [the gentleman] received the instruction to approach more closely. They asked him whether he possessed the fullness of humility and could prove it. He answered in the affirmative. What the girl sitting on the Leader's lap now did is such, that even the most superficial description of it would amount to a

punishable transgression against everything that goes by the name of morality.

Rather in the manner of the now defunct London scandal-sheet *News of the World*, which used to close its most lurid stories with the coy formula 'Our man made his excuses and left', Leipzig's *Unser Planet* tied up the narrative with the assurance that its informant, 'in whose heart the sense of shame was not yet extinguished', shrank from these horrors and fled from the scene, 'like Joseph did with Potiphar's wife'.[6]

The *Kritische Prediger-Bibliothek von Dr. Röhr* was less coy. It reported that the young girl had opened the novice's shirt front and 'playfully caressed his breasts':

> While he was obliged to endure this, he received the instruction to do the same with the holy girl. After these mutual titillations, known as the 'Seraphic pleasure', had taken place for some time, the holy girl made to take things further, but our unworthy young man found this too shameless and ran away.[7]

Like many other accounts, the *Prediger-Bibliothek* was fascinated by the elaborate hierarchical structure of the 'sect'. Its members included 'a large part of the nobility, many bourgeois and craftsmen, young and old women and used-up whores'. At their gatherings, the members were expected to demonstrate their unconditional subordination to the 'chief'. In the 'lower grades' of the sect, a 'used-up old female' would excite a young man sexually in the presence of witnesses, but then, when he reached the point where 'he must roughly enter her sexual parts', she would order him with their assistance to desist and push him back. Only in the 'higher grades', where older members gathered with young countesses, unmarried women and girls, was it permitted to practise the 'blending of the flesh'. In a droll concession to the ethics of good journalism, the article closed with a notice to the effect that the mothers of two young women had brought a suit against Count Finck von Finckenstein for claiming that their deceased daughters had died of 'lustful over-stimulation'. But the author added that the Provincial High Court had rejected this suit on the grounds that the results of the investigation were not yet available.[8]

Whether these claims should be taken seriously as descriptions of what actually happened within the Ebel circle is extremely doubtful. The formulaic character of the allegations, the prominence of hearsay, and their theatrical inversion of mid-nineteenth-century bourgeois sexual and social norms should give us pause. Groups alleged to be 'sects' were often accused of sexual excesses – this had always been one of the central strands of anti-sectarian discourse. Even of the modest auxiliary societies of the Berlin Society for the Promotion of Christianity among the Jews – innocuous small-town gatherings of pious artisans and their wives and daughters – it was claimed by local officials in the 1820s that their prayer meetings had produced an unacceptable level of arousal in the young women present.[9] When he was asked about the activities of the sect known as the 'Maldeniker' in the District of Labiau on the Kurisches Haff, an enormous lagoon on the Baltic coast, the local superintendent, who had never attended or observed their meetings, reported in 1822 that it was their custom to invite the women to confess in dark chambers, 'from which a few unhappy marriages had arisen, if the spouse was not a member of the sect'. We find similar speculations about sexual misbehaviour in the anti-Catholic discourses of the Culture Wars of the later nineteenth century.[10]

The *Mucker* story was picked up and discussed by newspapers across Germany. In February 1836 a poem entitled 'To the *Mucker*, a New Religious (?) Sect in the Land of Prussia' appeared on the first page of Leipzig's *Unser Planet*:

> You alone, you say, are the pious and good,
> Yet there you stand as Belial's brood,
> Spawn of the devil sprung straight from hell,
> Denouncing those folks who know you well
> Enough to see through your phoney game.
> Claiming to purge the flesh of its shame,
> The women and girls you groom and seduce;
> Your prayers are blasphemous acts of abuse,
> For – horror of horrors! – you set out to sow
> With thistles* the path where the innocent go.
> But beware, a judge is watching on high;
> And your Nemesis is drawing nigh.
> Hypocrisy's mask has fallen away.
> And your bestial faces are on display.
> You've lost forever the people's trust –
> For they speak of you everywhere now with disgust,
> Demanding a punishment swift and steep
> For wolves who go about dressed as sheep.[11]
>
> *Thistles (*Disteln*) is a play on the name Diestel.

Unser Planet was unusual in returning to the *Mucker* theme again and again with detailed articles and lampoons – all of them based on information from the anti-Ebelian camp.[12] But virtually all the mentions were hostile and the same core tropes and phrases were passed around from paper to paper. In an extended treatment of the Königsberg events, the Nuremberg-based *Allgemeine Zeitung von und für Bayern* noted that the *Mucker* circle of Königsberg had 'at last cast aside the veil that concealed its hideous nakedness and stands before us in all its pitifulness'.[13] The *Regensburger Zeitung* noted that the *Mucker* had pursued an aim that was good in itself, namely the purification of the flesh, but using means so repellent that even the most shameless could not hear of them without blushing.[14] The *Augsburger Postzeitung* reported that the 'conventicles' of the *Mucker* were attended by 'naked men and females, who were aroused to the point of the bursting with desire, but were expected to deny themselves the actual enjoyment'. Ebel and Diestel were described as 'the popes of the sect'.[15]

Ebel appears to have responded to these provocations with noteworthy calm and restraint. Diestel found it more difficult to keep his cool, but even he mostly maintained his self-control during these tribulations, though one observer reported rancorous exchanges when the hostile witnesses were actually confronted with the accused. But we can easily imagine what it meant to these men to be accused in print of having 'used religion as a fig-leaf for whore-mongering', or of presiding over sexual orgies at a time when their ongoing suspension from office and the circulation of so much calumny in print seemed to lend credibility to even the most outrageous accusations.

13.
Dr Sachs Accuses

No one did more to enrich the scandal around Ebel and Diestel with allegations of sexual misbehaviour than Dr Ludwig Wilhelm Sachs. Born in 1787 in Silesian Groß-Glogau, Sachs had come to Königsberg as a child with his parents. At the age of seventeen he gave up his apprenticeship with a local merchant and became a student of medicine, first in Königsberg and later at the universities of Berlin and Göttingen. Having taken his doctorate in Göttingen in 1812, he returned to Königsberg to serve as a senior physician in the city's hospitals, tending the masses of war wounded. In 1816 he submitted his *Habilitation*, a second and higher doctoral qualification on the subject of mental illnesses. By 1826, he had been appointed to a tenured professorship at the University of Königsberg. Sachs was a popular teacher and an industrious practitioner of his profession. He was also a prolific writer, though his books embodied a romantic, nature-philosophical approach to medicine, dense with metaphysical assumptions, that was already obsolete by the 1840s.[1]

We have already seen that Sachs initially sought Ebel's advice in the matter of his own conversion and that of his wife and son from Judaism to Christianity. Conversions of this kind were not uncommon in the Prussia of this era. Thanks to the Emancipation Edict of 1812, Jews living in the Prussian lands at the time of the promulgation of the Edict no longer suffered most of the civil disabilities that had burdened them in the past. They were declared henceforth to be 'natives' (*Inländer*) and 'citizens of the state' (*Staatsbürger*). But certain forms of discrimination remained: higher teaching roles, political offices and senior military ranks remained closed to Jews, who were urged to convert if they intended to pursue their careers to the highest levels. In this way, and despite the Edict of Emancipation, the Prussian state remained a missionary establishment in which the key organs of power, administration and education were imagined as Christian in character and public functionaries were not shy about applying conversionary pressure to Jewish citizens.

Yet there is no reason to suppose that Sachs's conversion was purely expedient. His metaphysical understanding of medicine resonated with the theosophical tone of the Ebel circle and he may also have been drawn to Ebel himself, of whom he later wrote that 'the notable gracefulness and attractiveness of his outer appearance [. . .] did not fail to make a pleasant impression'.[2] Certainly no one in Königsberg at that time knew better how to win people over to Christianity. Fanny Lewald, the daughter of a Jewish household, recalled a rainy afternoon in the early 1820s when Ebel spoke to her and her fellow students in such a compelling and evocative way of the birth of Christ that she felt 'a great happy movement in her heart' at the thought that, for the first time, 'Jesus had come to life, even for me'.[3] And we should note that the attraction between Sachs and Ebel was probably reciprocal, in the sense that preachers of Ebel's evangelical and proselytizing type were drawn to flawed individuals who offered themselves as 'converts' to practical faith and religious truth.

Sachs's technical works, which included a study of the therapeutic value of opium and a massive three-volume *Handbook of Practical Pharmacology* co-written with a colleague, were prolix and

Fanny Lewald, 1848. She knew nearly everyone involved in the *Muckerprozess*. Drawing by Wilhelm August Rudolf Lehmann.

derivative works with a short scholarly half-life. More revealing of Sachs's character and outlook is his *On Knowledge and Conscience: Talks for Doctors*, published in 1826, shortly after he had broken with the Ebel group. The book opens with a prickly foreword declaring that only someone with a malicious ulterior motive could possibly misunderstand the high-minded purpose of his pages:

> To assume such a motive in the reader, to infer it from the nastiness we see so much of in public criticism today, would not just be unfriendly, it would also be pointless, because there is no defence [no comeback] against malice. If someone has set out deliberately to misunderstand the book, will he feel obliged to understand this foreword properly?[4]

In the opening chapter, Sachs addresses his readers, young doctors, as trembling pilgrims making their way out into a dangerous world. The path is thorny. 'Darkness is encamped around [the newly graduated doctor] and it raises itself up like a tower as soon as he begins his journey.' But there is no reason for despair, for the young physician is armed with the power that God himself, the father of light, has given him. Around him, the creatures of darkness (*Düsterlinge*) whimper and rage at him, but he welcomes this as a sign that he is on the right track. He presses on in 'indestructible inner cheerfulness, invisibly connected with the Good Ones of past and present, under the all-powerful blessing of his heavenly father, until his day's work is done, and he is called across into the dwellings of peace'.[5]

Where others are content with superficial effects and 'phantastical games', the physician peers into the heart of existence, not with his outer eye, but with his 'inner eye, with the eye of the immortal spirit'. Through his studies he comes to understand the world 'as an altercation, a kind of chemical interaction between darkness and light'. He comes to see that sickness is not simply an organic state of affairs, but a form of evil, 'because in its essence and its root, [sickness] is an error, directed at the reversal of the divine order, [it is] the unfree and the ugly'. To work effectively against it, the young doctor must free himself from the 'admittedly well-meaning but always foolish zealotry [*Schwärmerei*] of believing that evil does not exist'. In other words, his research must penetrate to the root of evil, which must be 'grasped, broken and extirpated'. To achieve this, he will need not just knowledge and experience but the power of 'a moral personality that has become conscious in the truth'.[6]

The author's understanding of the doctor's calling could hardly be more exalted. The doctor who knows his profession, Sachs writes, 'will be seized by its sacred quality, for it is none other than to bring health through godly power, to rescue life from its fallen condition and to lead it back into peace with itself and to its original source'.[7] And as he pursues this high calling the physician will naturally find himself at battle with the 'worldlings' around him, lazy creatures easily provoked and offended by his quest for truth. The struggle will be especially intense when sexual factors are involved. The causes of illness must be exposed, Sachs writes, 'even when they lie in the domain of morality', and he must insist upon their elimination. In doing so he will vex and enrage 'The World', which 'absolutely does not want its sins and errors to be made known'.

The threat posed by sexual vice, Sachs announced, could scarcely be overstated. It wasn't just the victims themselves who paid the price, for in so many cases the 'poison [was also] thrown into future generations'. Illnesses of sexual origin were especially difficult to heal because they derived from 'the misuse of the noblest powers of the human being' – about one-fifth of all adults who died 'in the educated world and especially in cities' were 'direct or indirect victims of [sexual] vice'. Particularly vicious were the effects of masturbation, a hidden pandemic that was corroding the health of entire societies. This was a vice, Sachs wrote, 'against which doctors should struggle, and struggle victoriously. [. . .] The doctor should not lose himself in arcadian dreams when he stands in the hospital: he should know the enemy, recognize and attack him, he should not say: be at peace!' Sachs declared that he had himself already 'discovered several hundred cases of masturbation – at every level of extremity, at many different ages and with the most diverse consequences'. Almost never was the confession freely offered by the patient, mostly it had to be got at through cunning, in the manner of a 'difficult birth'. 'There was never any reason to doubt the truth of the confession, because I never called the thing by its name, rather I asked the children to tell me what they do *in secret*.' Thanks to this vigilance, Sachs reported, he had been able to save countless patients from unspeakable misery.[8]

Reading this book, one is struck not just by the author's

almost hallucinatory self-regard, but also by his hieratic understanding of the physician's role. The entire text is structured by moral polarities. The battle against disease is a battle with evil; an evil enabled and supported by indulgent 'worldlings' who refuse to understand the meaning and importance of the physician's holy work. He is a carrier of light and eternal truth making his way through a maelstrom of darkness and lies. The sources of Sachs's early attraction to Ebel and his circle are discernible here, but perhaps also the roots of the hatred Sachs would come to feel for the Ebelians after his departure from their company.

Sachs spoke out against Ebel before the Consistory and was recalled on several occasions to make statements before the court, evidence of the importance the investigating authority attached to his testimony. The protocols of those depositions do not survive, presumably because they were destroyed with the consistorial archive at the end of the Second World War, but on 15 July 1836, Sachs composed a long written statement. If he had voluntarily taken up his pen once again, he wrote, this was in the hope that his statement – coming as it did from a man who had written his second doctoral dissertation on mental illness – could 'be of use to the judge in a psychological perspective'.[9] What followed was an exceptionally hostile portrait of the key characters in the Ebel drama, a portrait that owed little to the categories or methodology of contemporary psychology. Ebel himself, Sachs reported, was the grandson of a fanatical old man with mystical leanings. His was an 'originally very talented nature', but one incapable of straightforward development. He was mentally very excitable and easily aroused, driven by a sense of special importance and drawn – possibly for hereditary reasons – to the hazy promises of theosophy. Because Ebel was work-shy and too lazy for research, he had 'never emerged from the condition of deepest ignorance' and had no experience of intellectual work of the kind Sachs himself had pursued. And this meant in turn that Ebel was 'entirely unprotected against inspirations [and] half-baked ideas'. Tired old errors that had been chewed over and spat out by many generations over and over appeared to Ebel in his naivety as fresh inspirations. No wonder he was attracted to the teachings of Schönherr, of whose life and thinking Sachs provided a parodic summary account.[10]

In Sachs's view, it was Ebel's encounter with Ida von der Groeben in 1817 that had set him on the road to the disasters that followed – Sachs was apparently unaware that Ida had in fact known Ebel since 1805, when her father engaged him as tutor to her two brothers.[11] His ascent into the milieu of the best East Prussian families unleashed the worst features of his personality. Ebel came to believe, Sachs claimed, that he was himself a member of the Trinity; he believed he had been present when the world was created. He came to believe he was the primordial fire entity and eventually that he was Christ himself – not the original Christ, but a completed version, because the first Christ was born of only one human being, whereas the completed Christ had to have two human parents. But Ebel was no fool – he confided these crazed delusions only to his innermost circle, Count Kanitz, Ida von der Groeben and Minna von Derschau, who later became Kanitz's wife – an observation that raises the question of how Sachs came to know of them.

The prominent role played by the women closest to Ebel was a particular focus of interest for Sachs. Three of them supposedly became Ebel's 'spiritual wives': Ida was his 'Light-wife'; Miss Emilie von Schrötter was his 'Darkness-wife', and his actual spouse – and mother of his children – came to be termed the 'envelope' or 'enclosure' (*Umfassung*). An important feature of the transactions that took place among members of the sect, in Sachs's view, was the sanctification through controlled forms of sexual intimacy in honour, as it were, of the primordial beings, whose essence was sexual. 'And so the acts [of purification] had to be sexual in character and one had to talk as they took place; for that is consciousness.' But sexual encounters had to be stopped before conception was accomplished. And the women involved in these rituals were expected first to deliver themselves of detailed sexual confessions itemizing their sinful desires and temptations, and thereby to enter a condition of subordination and dependency. This only applied to young women, because older or elderly women 'who were sexually no longer women', were in no need of this kind of 'correction'.[12]

Was the Ebel group a 'sect'? For Sachs, the answer was unequivocally yes. It was a sect, but not necessarily a Christian one. The pseudo-Christian teachings of Ebel were hopelessly entangled with the theosophical nonsense of Schönherr – there was no separating them. (This was Sachs's riposte to the statements made by Diestel and Ebel to the effect that they had never adopted Schönherr's teachings as a 'system'.) Ebel was not just the chief of the sect, he was its god, thought Sachs. His interactions with the women in his milieu were thoroughly immoral. But he was difficult to pin down, because, unlike the apostle Paul, he was not 'all things to all people' but rather a chameleon, a protean shape-changer, a seducer and deceiver. If one wanted to see how it all worked, one needed only take a look at the tract *Philagathos*, published by Ebel's detractor Ludwig August Kähler in 1823–4. The book captured precisely the inner workings of Ebelianism; the orgy-like scene at the end of the second volume might 'horrify and disgust' the reader, but it was not a fiction.

The most compelling passage in Sachs's statement relates to Minna von Derschau, a confidante of Ebel and later the wife of Count Kanitz. 'She had as the broadest foundation of her personality,' wrote Sachs, 'a strong sensuality, coupled with a very lively imagination unconstrained by even elementary instruction' – this was the doctor speaking: Minna had once been his patient. At the core of her being was 'a great warm-heartedness – she said herself that she tended to lustfulness'. Ebel had calmed her by making it clear to her that this was in itself no sin, provided it were not misused by the 'Enemy' (Satan). Minna became completely devoted to the preacher, wrote Sachs: 'it was with her that Ebel first practised the sexual purifications and, as Ebel told me, it was she who first mentioned and asked for them'. After he had put her through an extended period of purifications, Minna, 'a strongly sensual wench' who, thanks to Ebel's ministrations, 'had long been in a state of sexual arousal', was handed over to become the wife of Kanitz, a weak, servile and eunuch-like man who was scarcely a suitable partner for this spirited and highly sexed young woman. That was the power of Ebel, Sachs wrote: if he had said to Ida von der Groeben, 'Go to that man and give yourself to him as a woman', she would have done so without demur.[13]

How much of this was true? Was any of it true? Ebel, Diestel and their supporters all vehemently denied it. When the substance of Sachs's allegations became known, there were libel suits by those he had slandered, and by the relatives of the two deceased young women (Emilie von Schrötter and Minna von Derschau) whose posthumous reputations Sachs had besmirched. No corroborating evidence from other sources exists for Sachs's extraordinary portrait of the inner life of the 'sect'. And it is exceptionally hard to reconcile Sachs's claims about Ebel and Diestel with the consistorial files detailing their conduct, which was unblemished, or with the testimonies of the great number of parishioners who petitioned Carl von Altenstein, the Minister of Church Affairs, and even the king himself for the return of their beleaguered pastors and teachers.

Sachs, on the other hand, proved to be a complex witness to the events he had described. The physician had come to Ebel with a reputation for drunkenness and licentiousness. During his early years in the circle, he had penned long written confessions of his own rather garish sexual misdemeanours, which had circulated among the ladies close to Ebel. During the trial, the counsel to the accused called in statements from women who had been the patients of Dr Sachs or who had encountered him in the course of his professional activity; these reported Sachs's propensity to press unwanted intimacies upon the women in his care. A certain Fräulein Sophie Louise von Billerbeck, who knew Sachs as her family doctor, recalled how at the age of sixteen or seventeen, shortly after the death of her father, Sachs had cornered her in a doorway 'and kissed her in such a manner that he had pressed her head right back and stuck his tongue as far as he possibly could into her mouth'. Trembling with terror, she had stumbled into her mother's room and told her what had happened. Incredulous, her mother had suggested that Sachs might have intended by means of this operation to convey the Holy Spirit to her. Another witness, an unmarried woman by the name of Wilhelmine Krieger, reported that she had been caring for a sick friend in 1822, during which time Sachs was still closely associated with Ebel, when the doctor, who happened to be treating Wilhelmine's friend, 'kissed her passionately and asked her whether she would like to see him completely undressed and totally naked? which offer, however, she rejected.'[14]

A further witness, a convalescing widow by the name of von Schimmelpfennig, reported at length on an occasion in 1828 – after Sachs's breach with Ebel – when she asked the doctor to examine a 'sick spot' on the right side under one of her ribs. In order to do this, she had to open her dress, so that he, who was sitting opposite her, could see and investigate the 'sick' area. Her testimony is worth citing at length:

> At this point none of my carers were present. During this examination I became red in the face with embarrassment. Sachs embraced me, said: 'there is nothing serious to worry about', and kissed me. I gave him the benefit of the doubt; I thought it was his sympathy with my illness which had prompted him to give me a kiss. On the following day he was, probably because I had tolerated the kiss, of the opinion that I would tolerate yet more from him, and now he took me completely in his arms, and kissed me in a manner that one can only describe as lustful, in as much as he stuck his tongue into my mouth. But I still could not bring myself to dismiss Professor Sachs, because I had too high an opinion of his professional capability. And so I felt obliged to speak with him openly about this transaction because this encounter had clearly made me more ill, since in its aftermath I found the nights more difficult.
>
> I therefore asked him on the following morning when he visited me and found me bedbound, that I simply could not understand and did not believe that it could be pleasing to God if a person loved someone with such passion; (I called his behaviour 'love' because I wanted to spare his feelings.) He assured me, on the contrary, that Christians can never love each other enough, reached for the Bible and opened up a chapter on love. We could not come to an agreement, and I told him

that I would reproach myself in my conscience if I were to give myself to him as he appeared to wish, and that I had felt these compunctions already at night because I had let him kiss me.

As a consequence of this conversation, he declared that I was possessed by the devil. He sat down before my bed, made all kinds of gestures over my head and cried out quite loudly unintelligible words. I looked at him big-eyed with astonishment . . .[15]

At this point, very unfortunately, the file breaks off in mid-sentence. The following volume is missing. A look at the catalogue (*Findbuch*) drawn up by the Geheimes Staatsarchiv in 1909 reveals that an archival signature was originally assigned to the following volume, but that it never arrived or at least was never integrated into the archive's collection.[16] It is unlikely, in any case, that further statements from women who had been accosted by Sachs would do much to change the general picture.

Sachs's response to these revelations was angry and contemptuous but tends to reinforce the impression generated by the testimonies against him. Referring to the complaints of four women (whether these included any of the three women whose testimonies I have just cited is not clear) adduced by the defence, Sachs described the complainants as 'unhappy females [*Frauenzimmer*], all of them old, not especially well endowed, even physically disfigured persons':

> Some maids (very old maids incidentally) claim that I kiss like a debauchee! How are maids supposed to know something like that? [. . .] An ancient woman, the mother of several adult children, whom I saw for professional reasons alone, as a doctor, because she was suffering from an illness that caused her to

salivate excessively, says that I kissed her; to be honest, this could only have happened out of charity and in the spirit of self-denial . . .[17]

The psychoanalysis of dead persons is no straightforward matter, and we will never arrive at an unequivocal understanding of Sachs's behaviour. We do know that Finck von Finckenstein had projected onto Ebel the desire that Finckenstein had confided to his own wife Wilhelmine, namely that Ebel should be present when the couple made love. Perhaps a similar projective mechanism was in play when Sachs, who nearly everyone seems to have agreed was a troubled man, accused Ebel of outrages closely resembling his own behaviour when he managed to corner women (and not just older ones) in the seclusion of their homes.

Commissioner Adolf von Hake, the second most important provider of sexual innuendo against Ebel, also turned out to have a complex sexual history. Enquiries into his personal circumstances revealed that he had 'impregnated two girls out of wedlock'. The first, a young woman by the name of Johanne Kutsch, was the tutor of von Hake's daughter when the young woman became pregnant by him in 1830. According to a statement by a Dr Kniewel in Danzig, she had been abandoned by von Hake after her confinement. With the help, in part, of Ebel and Diestel, she was able at last to secure another position as house tutor, while her child, without any support on the part of the father, was brought up through the help of friends of the young mother. The second impregnated girl, a certain Sophie Frederike Wilhelmine Raubusch, was the daughter of a master tailor in the town of Preußisch Holland (today Pasłęk in Poland). Her friendly contact with von Hake's daughter, a girl of the same age, had given him the opportunity to see Sophie frequently. By persuading her that he intended to divorce his wife, from whom he was already separated, and marry her, von Hake succeeded in inducing Sophie to sleep with him. This intimate relationship became the occasion for disagreements between the girl and her foster parents in the city. They persuaded the long-suffering Frau von Hake, who was aware that her husband had promised to marry Sophie, to accept her into the von Hake household. It was during her residence in his home that von Hake surprised Sophie in her bedroom and impregnated her.[18]

Ebel, Diestel and their counsel argued that these revelations raised doubts about the probity of the prosecution's witnesses. The court disagreed. The finding on Sachs is no longer extant, but in the matter of von Hake, the court was happy to accept that as he had done much to mend his ways since these earlier depredations had taken place, his testimony should now be trusted. A senior church functionary, a Church Superintendent by the name of Dreist, who was asked to testify on von Hake's credibility, conceded that he had never encountered a person whose 'attitude and conduct' gave him 'such good reason to avoid and flee him'. There had been a time in von Hake's life when 'his conduct was extremely immoral, so that he forewent the trust of all respectable and honourable people'. But in recent times there had been a marked turn to the better. 'Since these days my business often brings me into personal contact and friendly connection with him, I have also been a witness [to occasions] when he spoke with disgust of his earlier life [. . .] and takes pleasure in the transformation that has occurred in his character and conduct'. In short: the past was the past. 'If I wish to speak of the present and of the time when von Hake acted as a witness in the Ebel case, I have to admit that I have nothing negative to say about his conduct.'[19]

14.
The End of the Road

From the East Prussian Consistory to the Presidency of the Province of Prussia, to the Ministry of Church Affairs and the judiciary in Königsberg and Berlin, the official mind of the Kingdom of Prussia had composed itself against the two beleaguered clergymen. Already in November 1835, Carl von Altenstein was writing to Theodor von Schön that the two men would have to go to court – the matter was too serious and must be cleared up.[1] In a firmly worded letter to Pastor Diestel, who had complained of irregularities in the conduct of the investigation, the minister – who was no theologian! – insisted on the irreconcilability of the doctrine of the two primordial beings with church teaching and explained that Diestel would have to join Ebel in the dock, not just because he shared Ebel's views, but because it would be necessary to check his fitness for further pastoral work.[2] When Diestel, who had already been fined heavily for insulting Finckenstein, wrote to Altenstein in June 1836 denouncing Theodor von Schön and the Consistory, the minister responded by ordering that Diestel be prosecuted before the Provincial High Court in Königsberg. (The prosecution took place and resulted in a sentence to six months of fortress arrest.)[3] In 1814, when Ebel faced a campaign of harassment from the church authorities in Königsberg, the central government in Berlin, in the shape of the theologian Friedrich Schleiermacher, had come to his rescue. This time there would be no protective intervention from the capital.

Ebel and Diestel were not friendless. Their closest associates peppered the provincial and central government with letters and tried to launch suits of their own. The widow Consentius née Lorck wrote to Altenstein complaining that Count Finck had besmirched the good name of her deceased daughter, who was one of the two girls Finckenstein claimed had died of excessive sexual arousal. In fact she had died of a respiratory illness. Her mother demanded – in vain – that Finckenstein be punished for this calumny.[4] We have seen that Ida von der Groeben passionately defended her friends Ebel and Diestel, denounced the lies and manipulations of Finckenstein, and demanded that the investigation be halted forthwith. In December 1835, Carl Benjamin Waschke, a teacher at the Royal Orphanage and the Teachers' College in Königsberg, wrote a petition to the king in which he praised Ebel and Diestel as men 'suffused with the most glowing and yet reasonable passion for the purposes of God'.[5] Count Kanitz also protested to the Consistory and to Minister Altenstein.[6] Diestel himself wrote a predictably spirited sixty-page letter to the Provincial High Court, urging it to take up his case against Finckenstein for the slanders he had endured.[7] In a letter to Altenstein and his colleague, Interior Minister Gustav von Rochow, Diestel denounced the slanders of Sachs and von Hake, complained of the partisanship of the President of the Province of Prussia, Theodor von Schön, and requested that the correspondence between Schön and the authorities be made available to their advocate so that they could defend themselves against the campaign mobilized against them.[8]

Even the confirmation candidates of the Old City Church got active in defence of their preacher. Their petition to the monarch, filed on 17 November 1835, when news of the investigation was still fresh, opened with the words:

> With deeply felt trust and full of awe we draw near the throne of our Prince and place our urgent request in the fatherly heart of our dear king: Give us back our beloved teacher!!

The text of the petition announced that the signatories were 'seized with the deepest pain', because 'maliciously invented lies and calumnies' had prompted the Royal Consistory to suspend their religious instructor:

> ... we feel abandoned, we who have been robbed of our fatherly friend and teacher, and on many occasions the words have been heard from our midst: 'I'm going to write to our king', and as this could not remain an empty word, a number of us decided to pour out our deepest wish and warmest longing before our beloved Prince. Oh, if only we were capable of depicting in vivid colours the piety and the love of doctor Ebel, a love that suffuses everything with happiness, that awakens every heart to good things, and to convey before your majesty's eye an image of a demeanour that seems touched by God. Words are incapable of expressing it [. . .] the hours in which our dear teacher introduced us to the will of God were the most beautiful of our lives thus far, to be outdone only by the beautiful hour in which our teacher is restored to us through the grace and justice of your majesty.[9]

The petition carries eighty-seven signatures. A petition to Frederick William III filed on 1 September 1836 by 'members of the Old City Parish and listeners to [the sermons of] Archdeacon Dr Ebel' notes that 'nearly a year has passed since malice, envy

The End of the Road

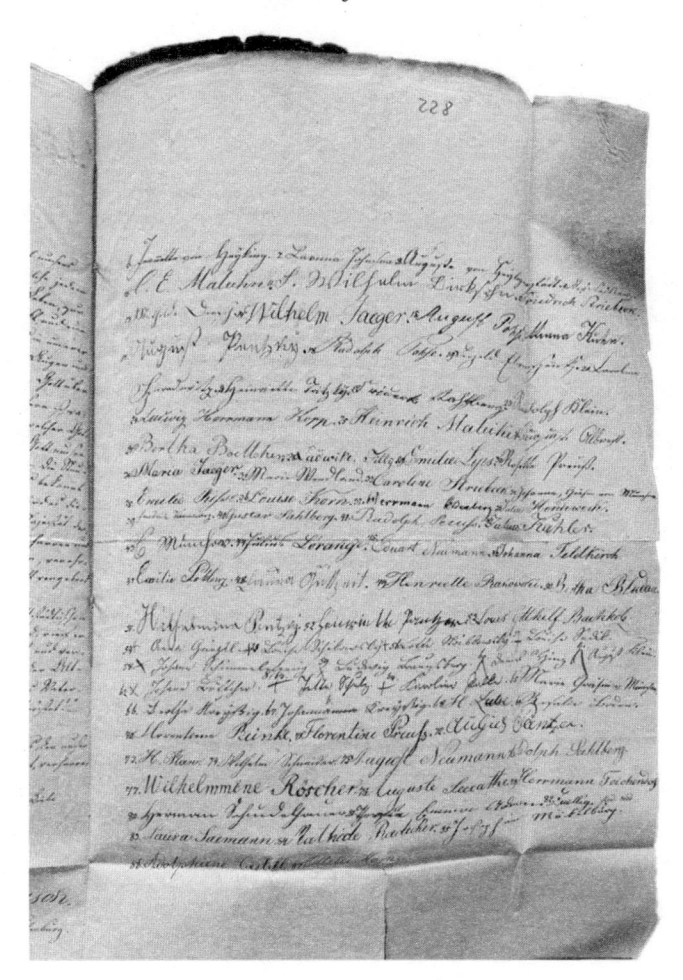

Signatures attached to a petition from members of the Ebel congregation to King Frederick William III imploring the king to return their 'beloved teacher', Johannes Ebel, to them, 17 November 1835.

and malevolence robbed us of our dear and truly faithful teacher and pastor'. Many families, who owed 'their domestic happiness exclusively to this faithful teacher and found [his] support in times of trouble', felt this loss deeply. The signatories had

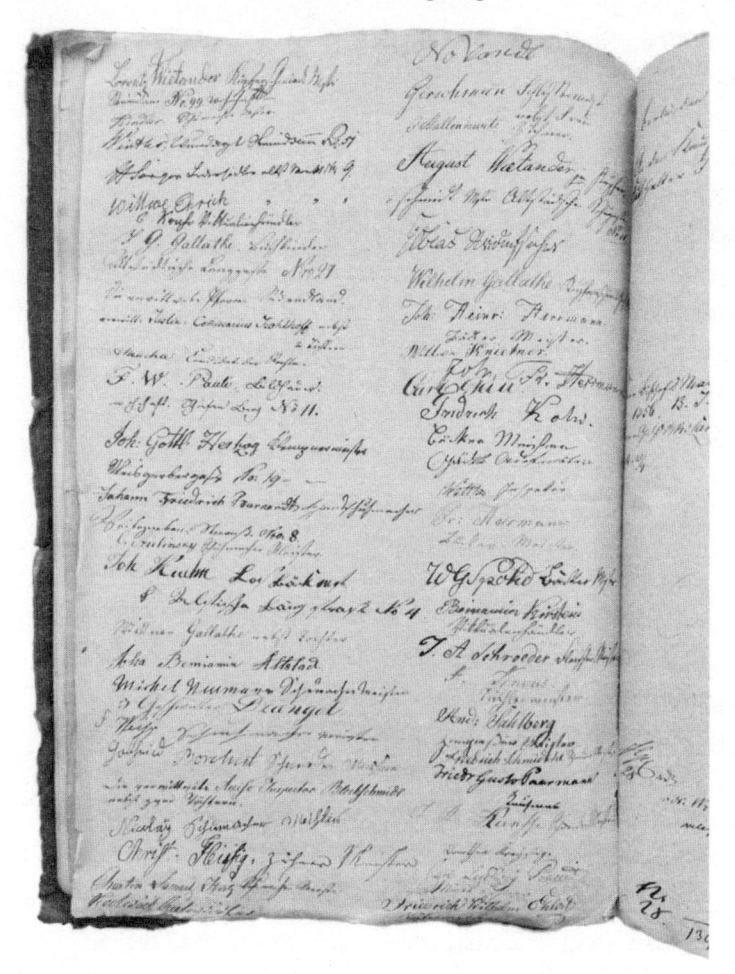

Signatories to a petition by 'Members of the Old City Congregation and Listeners to Archdeacon Dr Ebel' to King Frederick William III of Prussia requesting the return of Dr Ebel to teaching and pastoral duties, 14 September 1836.

been following closely the progress of the criminal investigation, which had ended two months earlier: 'we are not unaware that it has not been possible to prove any of the shameful lies invented by a cunning hatefulness against Archdeacon Dr Ebel, he must therefore have been vindicated – all the more urgent is our request that his vindication be made known . . .'. The professions listed alongside the names of the more than fifty signatories reveal an interesting social profile: merchants, accountants, bookkeepers, grocers, a leather dealer, bookbinders, a sculptor, a master plumber, master shoemakers and their journeymen, various functionaries, apprentice coppersmiths, many master bakers and tailors, a tin-smith, a master potter and a music teacher, plus a sprinkling of widows, some of whom also signed in the name of their daughters. As this list suggests, Ebel's teaching and preaching resonated not just among the women of the best houses of the land, but also in an urban but not urbane milieu of skilled craftsmen and local service-providers.[10]

It was all in vain. On 15 August 1839, nearly four years after the beginning of the investigation into the activities of Ebel and Diestel, the Royal Cameral Court in Berlin at last produced a judgment. It stated that Ebel was guilty of premeditated breach of duty and of having founded an 'illegal sect', that he was to be suspended permanently from his office as archdeacon and preacher at the Old City Church (he had been suspended temporarily since the beginning of the investigation), and disqualified from holding any public offices in the future. He was to be conveyed to a correctional institution and confined there until his 'improvement' could be determined. Diestel was also found guilty of premeditated breach of duty, suspended permanently from office as preacher at the Haberberg Church, and likewise disqualified from holding any further public offices. The two men were liable for the costs of the investigation.[11]

This was a bitter outcome for the two defendants and the people who supported them. To be sure, the judgment of 15 August 1839 acquitted the two men of all of the more lurid accusations brought by their denouncers. The claims of sexual misconduct brought by Sachs, von Hake, Finckenstein and others were reported in the judgment but not upheld. On the other hand, the rejection of these claims was not integrated into the text of the judgment. We don't know why the judge acted in this way: he may have feared that officially denouncing calumnies as such in the text of the judgment would open the door to further lawsuits against the prosecution witnesses, the very people who had helped the authorities to secure this outcome. As Ebel's friend, the lawyer Count Kanitz, later observed, this omission placed the judgment at odds with the principle expressed in section 488 of the criminal code, according to which the infractions of which the defendant has been either acquitted or found guilty should all be named individually in the judgment.[12] And this created an asymmetry in the text: the innuendos received yet another airing but were not categorically denounced as lies in the part of the statement that mattered most. This was a serious blow to the rights and interests of the defendants, because it meant that people could keep hinting darkly at the persistence of accusations that remained unaddressed.

In the absence of any proven crimes against sexual morality, the Royal Cameral Court confined itself to charges relating to the illegal foundation of a sect. Even this conviction was far from straightforward. Prussian law provided very little guidance on what a 'sect' was and precious little in the way of instruments for the suppression of 'illegal sects', should they arise. The Prussian General Code of 1794 merely stated that a person was punishable if he or she founded a sect 'whose doctrines openly attacked the veneration of God' or 'led the people onto the path to vice'. But neither of these criteria was met. The court itself dismissed the allegations relating to vice

The End of the Road

and neither Ebel nor Diestel could reasonably be accused of 'attacking the veneration of God'. This aporia explains one of the strangest features of the judgment of 1839, namely that in justifying its authority to punish Ebel for the crime of founding a sect, it reached for the so-called 'Religion Edict' of 1788, a royal ordinance – issued at the height of the Enlightenment, and highly controversial even in its own time – to protect the officially recognized religious denominations from the spread of deist and ultra-rationalist theological teachings that supposedly threatened their cohesion. 'The Religion Edict', the judgment stated at folio 196, 'was absolutely right in forbidding clergymen all communications and even the cultivation of heterodox doctrines'. It is true that this edict did allow the authorities to act against clergymen who took excessive liberties with official doctrine – the problem was that in 1794 it was superseded by the Prussian General Law Code, which did not just assure every clergyman of his freedom of conscience, but also suspended all existing 'general Edicts and Ordinances', including the Religion Edict of 1788.[13] That the judge should have seen fit to invoke this outlandish and obsolete piece of law for service against Ebel was surely a sign of desperation.

After publication of the judgment, Ebel and Diestel decided to appeal. They could not have known that the tide was about to turn in their favour. The old king, Frederick William III, died in 1840, along with his faithful servant *Kultusminister* Altenstein. The new king, Frederick William IV, was much friendlier to evangelical and pietist forms of spirituality than his father had been, and so was the new Minister of Church Affairs, Friedrich Eichhorn, who replaced the decidedly rationalist Altenstein. The disciplining urge that had driven the campaign against non-conformist religion slackened.

Ebel and Diestel attempted to widen the scope of the

A Scandal in Königsberg

investigation by requesting that Theodor von Schön's correspondence with the Consistory, the Ministry of Church Affairs and Minister Altenstein be produced and placed in the hands of the court, so that they could show how their enemies had connived against them. The request was ignored. No one wanted to suck the powerful Oberpräsident of East Prussia into a further round of skirmishes over the *Mucker* of Königsberg. On 2 February 1842 the High Court of Appeal of the Cameral Court in Berlin published its judgment. The accused, it stated, were 'not to be sentenced to cashiering [Cassation] and disqualification from all public offices on account of *premeditated breach of duty*, but on account of the *negligent breach of professional duty*' – a less serious charge. The dismissal of the two men from their respective clerical posts was upheld. On the other hand, Ebel's sentence to confinement was quashed and he was 'acquitted of the accusation of foundation of a sect'. The case relating to the foundation of an 'illegal sect' had always been weak: Ebel and Diestel had called themselves Lutherans or Christians; they had never directly challenged the authority of the Union Church or of its doctrines; they both denied having adopted or promulgated the thoughts of Schönherr in the form of a 'doctrine' (*Lehre*) or 'system'.[14]

Perhaps more importantly, the new judgment corrected the public record on the question of Ebel's personal morality. It stated unequivocally that Ebel was an 'upright man of immaculate purity of morals', whose 'entire domestic situation [had] been identified by everyone who was close to him as free of fault and highly respectable'. This was an improvement, and it certainly amounted to a disavowal of the worst features of the first judgment. But it was scarcely the encompassing exoneration that the two men and their friends hoped for. Ebel initially moved into a small house purchased for him with donations from supporters, but later he left Königsberg and resettled with Ida von der Groeben in Ludwigsburg in the Grand Duchy of Baden, where they were later joined by a few faithful Ebelians. Ebel wrote a few further tracts elaborating his understanding of the Schönherr cosmogony, but these did not attract much notice and are described in one much later account as among the 'most confused and least enjoyable texts that have ever been printed'.[15] He died on 18 August 1861.

Diestel disappeared from public view. Even Fanny Lewald, who had known him well and was one of the best-informed observers of the whole affair, had no idea what became of him after the trial.[16] The last sign of life from him was a letter to the Königsberg Consistory requesting their permission to administer the blessing for the confirmation of his seriously ill daughter. When this small concession was granted, he replied in a trembling hand with effusive expressions of gratitude.[17] He died on 20 July 1854.

15.
Closing Thoughts

Reason and Unreason

Henry Kissinger once quipped that the quarrels among academics are only so bitter because the stakes in contention are so small. Whether this is true of academics is doubtful, but it was certainly not true of the people swept up in the scandal around Ebel and Diestel. They behaved as they did because they came to believe that the stakes were very large indeed. What was all the fuss about? To this question, the liberal press gave an unequivocal answer. It was about the struggle between reason and fanaticism, between rationalism and the darkness of sectarian obscurantism. One contemporary writer spoke in suggestive terms of the 'despoiling of reason'.[1] Here was a neat rubric under which to file away the troubles in Königsberg. Whatever Ebel and Diestel were or were not saying in private to their closest associates, their spirituality was clearly out of sync both with the doctrinally austere orthodoxy of the conservative clergy and with the fashionable theological rationalism of the era. At a time when the government had stepped up its vigilance against separatists and sectarians of all types, the eccentric flavour of their teachings might even have appeared politically suspect, especially if it seemed to challenge the legitimacy of on Church, viewed by its supporters as the rational solution to the plurality of religious sub-cultures that had flourished in turn-of-the-century Prussia.

In the struggle between light and darkness, the Provincial Governor of Prussia, Theodor von Schön, viewed himself as a champion of the light. Like many of his contemporaries, he described the Ebelians as *Finsterlinge*, or 'darklings'. In a letter to the Minister of Church Affairs, Friedrich Eichhorn, he described the religious enthusiasm cultivated by the Ebelians as a form of *Pietisterey* or pietistic excess. Its teachings were laughable: how could one take seriously a doctrine claiming that at the beginning of time 'two enormous eggs or balls are supposed to have swum around *in vacuo* [. . .] from whose intimate union the world and everything that is the world originated'?[2]

For the Hegelian philosopher Karl Rosenkranz, a close friend of Schön and a professor at the University of Königsberg, the scandal turned on the tension between reason and imagination. The stronger the grip of reason was in any particular place or individual mind, the more tempestuously would imagination rise up against it. Isaac Newton, the great mathematician, Rosenkranz pointed out, had also been 'an abstruse oracle of the apocalypse'. Humphrey Davy, the brilliant chemist, composed poems and was tormented by the wildest dreams, which he wrote down. The French, and especially the Parisians, were notorious for their reasonableness, but were also the sponsors of every swindle. Charles Fourier had started off perfectly sensible and ended up as mad as a March hare. 'It's much the same with us here in Königsberg,' Rosenkranz observed. 'We are very sensible, but we also have imagination.' Imagination was an essential and valuable faculty, but when it turned in on itself, when it ceased to test its sustainability under broad daylight, when it grew and began to brood, imagination was prone to become 'fantastical' – when this happened, it forsook the quest for ideal beauty that was its proper objective and indulged instead in 'oddities, in the embellishment of details, which at first manifest a certain coherence, but with time drift apart and lose definition'.[3] This was what had happened, Rosenkranz claimed, in the case of Ebel, Diestel and the unlettered bard Johann Heinrich Schönherr.

There was a certain irony in this because the roots of the Ebel movement, if it was a movement, lay in the aspiration to reconcile the scriptural content and moral teachings of Christianity with human reason.[4] We have seen that as a child Ebel had been encouraged to contemplate the word of scripture 'with sacred awe'. But as an adolescent and a young adult he had found that faith in the word of the Bible alone did not suffice to ward off the doubts and counter-arguments of his teachers and fellow pupils. In Schönherr's teachings, Ebel saw a means of bringing revealed religion into harmony with a reason founded upon observations from nature. Only a biblical faith reinforced by philosophy would be capable of dismantling the resistance of mainstream Christians to revealed religious truth – a task that appeared especially urgent in Königsberg, renowned both for its association with Kantian philosophy and for the rationalist flavour of its theology and governance. The attraction of Schönherr's writings, Diestel explained, lay precisely in their 'genuinely philosophical [*ächt philosophischen*]' character. Schönherr's thought represented the cutting edge of contemporary philosophical speculation; it was Schelling's 'final metamorphosis of philosophy'; it was:

> The only possible way of arriving at the famous *crux philosophorum* [puzzle of the philosophers], the *salto mortale* of philosophy, the transition from the infinite to the finite.[5]

Closing Thoughts

The pamphlet that Ebel and Diestel published together in 1837 to explain their views bore the telling title: *Understanding and Reason in Alliance with God's Revelation (Verstand und Vernunft im Bunde mit der Offenbarung Gottes)*. In his own contribution to this volume, Ebel told his readers that he had initially gravitated to Schönherr because he believed the latter had found 'a way of bringing the utterances of the Bible and its entire content into harmony with proofs derived from reason in a manner that was persuasive and invincible against the barbs of the mockers'. The good news from Schönherr, wrote Ebel, was that reason and biblical revelation stood in harmony with each other, and that there was a person on Earth (Schönherr) who had succeeded in mediating between them.[6]

This was not the 'reason' preferred by Schön, of course: Ebel's was not a 'religion within the boundaries of reason' in the Kantian sense, but rather a reason within the boundaries of religion. Reason, in his thinking, was not the precondition and legitimate test of belief, but the handmaiden and tool of religious faith. Ida von der Groeben captured this view of the matter when she observed in a letter to the king's younger son, Prince William of Prussia, that only the 'reasoned understanding of the Bible using the key supplied by the recognition of the two original entities' was capable of restoring nominal Christians of the modern type to a faith in the truth of the Bible.[7]

Impartiality

The attachment to reason was more than an abstract commitment. It was a mode of comportment with a strong performative dimension. Even Sachs, the most malicious confabulator of innuendo against the two accused clergymen, opened his statement to the court of 15 July 1836 with the words: 'A great many questions have been placed before me and answered by me conscientiously' and 'without the slightest personal excitement [*ohne die mindeste persönliche Erregtheit*]'.[8] In his communications with Altenstein, Theodor von Schön was always at pains to make it clear that he was on neither side of the controversy and that his actions were motivated exclusively by cool-headed and neutral assessments of the situation. Writing to the minister about an angry letter of complaint that Diestel had sent to Altenstein, Schön said: 'In response to passionate outbursts of this type, I merely infer that they stem from a partisan mind open to any form of defence and therefore leave them be in the confidence that I have done my duty.'[9] When Ida von der Groeben, Schön's sister-in-law, sent him a long letter of complaint and reproach, he responded with a lofty gesture:

> Dear Ida! Your letter of 25th of this month only reached me this morning and now I have opened it and read the first page I am obliged to reply to you as follows. I will always extend my hand to [you as] my sister[-in-law], because I am persuaded that you would do the same for me. However, as I see from the first page of your letter, you are writing to me in connection with the Ebel affair, on which for official reasons I can accept no communications without passing them to the official record. I have forbidden Count Finckenstein any discussion of this matter and I have asked him not to visit me until the matter is concluded. So I am sure you will understand that I will neither read nor keep your letter. My position requires the highest neutrality, *as difficult as this often is for me.*[10]

Closing Thoughts

Whether Schön was really as impartial as he claimed is, as we have seen, open to doubt. Ida von der Groeben certainly did not think so. In her letter she attacked him for his ruthless support of the campaign of persecution raised against her friend and even against herself. Schön, she wrote, had opened his ear to her slanderers and endorsed the insistent libelling of her name. He had gravely offended against 'the seriousness and weightiness of [his] civic office, which calls for the greatest sagacity and the most conscientious shunning of one's own prejudices and antipathies'. Schön, Ida wrote, had embraced accusations against people he knew – including Ebel and herself – people whose outlook, nature and way of acting he himself knew well, people who, over the years, had earned his respect. Worse, he had drawn these accusations from people he did *not* respect and of whom he had often spoken disparagingly:

> I know you, dear Schön, and I know that it is not an evil heart, a heart that seeks evil, that has led you so deeply into error, but nor is it a good heart, a heart that selflessly and disinterestedly seeks the good . . . [I know] that your character is not a hard character, but nor is it a firm one and [I know] that you became entangled in a great act of self-deception, that you lacked true judgement about others too, that you exposed yourself to the manipulation of all of those who either take pride in their own weakness, or for reasons of malice knowingly try to use the weakness of others, and especially of influential persons to achieve self-interested or even malicious objectives.[11]

Other Ebelians were just as scathing. Ida's sister Eveline von Bardeleben argued that the entire scandal had been engineered by Schön after his meeting with Finckenstein at the Danzig Provincial Diet, that it was Schön who orchestrated the choice and presentation of prosecution witnesses, turned down the requests from pro-Ebel witnesses to be heard by the Consistory and the court, and 'opened the protocols to every absurdity that could find a way of disguising itself as an accusation'.[12] For Count Kanitz, it was clear that the Consistory had abjectly failed to do its duty, namely to be impartial and to protect the individuals under its purview against the calumnies of their enemies.[13]

These were partisan perspectives, of course, from people at the centre of the trouble around Ebel. But in retrospect, most of their objections appear well founded, given the character of Schön's interventions in the investigation. His reports revealed 'a strong dependence on more or less anonymous sources' and a yawning ignorance of the theological dimension of the issues raised by Ebel's work. Schön was careful not to associate himself officially with the detail of the sexual slanders circulating against Ebel and his followers, but he spoke suggestively to his senior colleagues of the 'disgusting' excesses taking place among the Ebelians and no one did more to bolster the credibility of Dr Sachs as a 'witness' of what had transpired among them.[14] When it became known during the criminal trial that Dr Kähler of the Prussian Consistory was the anonymous author of an article in the *Allgemeine Kirchenzeitung* that sided against the two accused clergymen, Schön defended Kähler on the grounds that he had always demonstrated the most scrupulous neutrality and argued that no disciplinary measures were necessary.[15]

Even in Berlin there were those who had doubts about the impartiality of the investigation. Altenstein, the then Minister of Church Affairs, reacted sceptically to a number of Schön's early complaints, correcting him on points of fact.[16] And in an interesting Cabinet Order of 26 April 1836 to Altenstein and

Interior Minister von Rochow, Frederick William III expressed his concern about the failure of the censorship authorities to suppress the circulation of reports likely to prejudice the outcome of the investigation and ruin the reputation of the accused before a verdict had been reached. He urged the two ministers to be vigilant lest further such breaches occur.[17] Even more strikingly, the monarch copied this Cabinet Order to the two accused clergymen, together with a note in which he insisted on the fundamental fairness of the process but also reminded them that the investigation had been taken out of the hands of the Königsberg authorities, a comment that suggested awareness of the adverse climate Ebel and Diestel faced in their own town.[18]

The Public Sphere

The press and the circulation of rumours were central to the unfolding of the scandal around Ebel and Diestel. 'When I came to Königsberg,' Theodor von Schön told Altenstein in the summer of 1835, 'I found the public very worked up against the Ebelians.'[19] 'The public here is extremely agitated about this matter,' he wrote to Altenstein a month later.[20] In a letter to the King in October 1835, Altenstein explained that it was the pressure of public opinion that had made it necessary to launch an investigation in Königsberg.[21] Hostile treatments of the scandal spoke of 'general agitation' and a bitterness erupting from 'the lower strata of the people', so that the friends of Ebel, whenever they appeared in public experienced 'unheard-of mockery by the mob'. Again and again, the people driving the investigation referred to public opinion as something beyond their control, an exogenous pressure on decision-makers, a popular tribunal that it was perilous to ignore.

And yet a closer look at how the events unfolded reveals that popular opinion was not the driver of the scandal around Ebel and Diestel but to a considerable extent a function of how it was managed. The Ebelians were intensely aware of this. 'Even before the trial began,' wrote the Ebelian Eduard von Hahnenfeld, 'the people driving it had already won over that lady known as "public opinion".' The 'mockery of the mob' that greeted the Ebelians wherever they went was an invention, as was the 'bitterness' against them supposedly percolating up from the lower classes. The 'fiction of popular outrage', Hahnenfeld wrote, was invented as 'a trump that could be played' in order to overcome any doubts the judges might have about coming to a guilty verdict.[22] And once the media had drawn a thoroughly false picture of the inner life of the group around Ebel, this became a kind of reality in its own right, proliferating through the papers and journals across the German states, and even into handbooks of theology and encyclopaedias of religious history.[23] In any case, it made no sense in the Königsberg of Theodor von Schön to speak of the President of the Province of Prussia as operating under the pressure of public opinion. Although a courageous advocate of constitutionalism against the stodgy, neo-absolutist Berlin monarchy, Schön was a progressive of the authoritarian type who had consistently made robust use of censorship in order to shape and mute public opinion. Throughout the 1830s he subjected the Provincial Diet to strict control through the censor's office.[24] The seething of rumour around the Ebel scandal in the provincial press was thus policy, not the *force majeure* of an autonomous public sphere. In a hostile but acute characterization, Eveline von Bardeleben observed that:

Closing Thoughts

... no effort was spared to infect and mislead so-called 'public opinion', which holds itself to be the truest guarantor of lawfulness, in order to use it as a basis and support for the agitation of spirits, and thereby acquire retrospective pretexts for an official attack. Where the justification for coercive measures was lacking, the arousal of the populace was supposed to serve instead.[25]

The concept of the 'public sphere', as Jürgen Habermas so influentially defined it, possessed from the outset a secular or post-religious character. In the critical, dialogical, rational, 'bourgeois' and liberal public sphere theorized by Habermas, religion appeared as the remnant of a traditional and in essence already obsolete social order. The exclusion of religion from the public sphere, imagined in its turn as the fruit of processes of societal and economic modernization, appeared to be warranted by the historical sources. After all, it was a defining feature of those bodies that were taken to constitute the emergent public sphere – eighteenth-century reading clubs, Masonic lodges and patriotic, musical or scientific societies – that religion, at least in principle, was barred from entry, on the grounds that it would divide members against each other and thus endanger sociability.[26] And these biases within the sources were amplified by an ideal-typical schema in which the public sphere was defined in terms of its function as a 'space of reason-giving', whereas religion figured as inherently irrational and authoritarian.[27]

One might even admire the skill with which the city's elite helped to build the negative publicity generated by the scandal and the subsequent trial. But it cannot be said that the publicity exemplifed the 'reason-giving' virtues of the Habermasian public sphere, or that it created a climate in which 'the best argument won'. What we have here is not a triumphant demonstration of the Habermasian ideal type, but one rather dark – if far from definitive – glimpse of the historical conditions in which the idea of an exclusively liberal and rational public sphere was born.

Sex

Had Ebel and the people around him merely been accused of admixing their Lutheran spirituality with scraps of esoteric cosmogony, it is hard to imagine either that the scandal around them would have escalated as it did or that the authorities would have succeeded in disgracing the two clergymen and driving them out of public life. We have seen that the provincial church authorities had tried to winkle Ebel out of office in 1814 on much less sensational charges, but had failed to do so. In the 1830s, by contrast, rumours of sexual depravity lay at the heart of the accusations. As the supporters of Ebel never tired of pointing out, there was a counter-intuitive quality to this trade in sexual rumour, both because the two men were known to be steady and sexually reserved figures and because the perversities alleged and hinted at by the accusers and in the journals were comprehensively dismissed in both the first and second judgments.

Yet it was sex that gave wings to the scandal. There was a time when nobody in the city seemed interested in talking about anything else than the unexpectedly lurid lives of the *Mucker*. Fanny Lewald, who personally knew Ebel and his closest associates to be people of impeccable morals, recalled how swiftly scraps of news, hearsay and rumour thickened around the trial. First there was the news that local personalities had denounced the two clergymen to the authorities:

Closing Thoughts

And then rumours about the inner goings-on of the Ebel congregation entered public awareness [. . .] These rumours grew from day to day [. . .] It was said that the husband of a highborn lady to whom Ebel had made an indecent proposal had started the process of uncovering his activities, and the more excited people in general became about the whole affair, the more actively they applied their imagination to adding even worse things to the details that gradually became known about the doctrines and exercises of the sect.[28]

The fact that everyone in Königsberg knew Ebel and Diestel by sight, the fact that their official conduct reports had remained unblemished for many years, did little to slow the circulation of this traffic in rumours and half-truths.

By 1842, when the second trial came to an end, interest in the Ebel scandal had ebbed. The second judgment made it abundantly clear that there was no substance to the sexual allegations against the principal parties. In the light of this fact, the garishness of the inventions is all the more remarkable. Choirs of naked women, polygamous unions, the sexual stimulation of adolescents, kisses so obscene that to describe them would incur legal sanction, a towering hierarchy of ranks requiring lurid rites of initiation. That these fantasies generated pleasure must be part of the reason for their swift proliferation. But what is interesting about them is how they invert the utopia of the progressive imagination of that era, a world composed of compact clan and household units governed by independent, newspaper-reading, authoritative men. That 'the sleep of reason engenders monsters' is proverbial. This is often taken to mean that the monsters run riot when reason is disempowered – in Goya's powerful and disturbing image, they can be seen gathering behind the sleeping figure in the foreground.

Francisco da Goya, *El sueño de la razon produce monstruos* (*The sleep of reason produces monsters*). Etching from the series, 'Los Caprichos', 1799.

But the meaning of the maxim is ambiguous, especially in Spanish, because the word *sueño* can also mean 'dream'. In the context of the *Muckerprozess* of 1830s Königsberg, one can read Goya's adage in exactly this way: namely that the dreams of reason can themselves be monstrous. The grotesques conjured up by the press (at the behest of the provincial authorities) were not images of what had actually transpired around Ebel and Diestel, but the fantastical inversions of liberal ideals.

The Queerness of Ebel

At the heart of the social universe of the progressive elites in Königsberg was the complementarity between forms of male and female behaviour imagined as stable and polarized. In his reflections on 'sexual difference', published in 1837, the Königsberg philosopher Karl Rosenkranz – a close friend of Theodor von Schön who often attended the soirées at his residence and was asked by the court trying Ebel and Diestel to submit an expert opinion on the documents[29] – insisted on the many binary oppositions. On one side: the 'delicate, tender and curved' forms of women; on the other: the 'sharp, energetic and taut' forms of men. 'Woman' was bound to 'nature' by her very constitution; 'man' was free from 'nature' by the same token. Pregnancy and the nursing of children bound women to the safety of enclosed spaces, confining them to an eternal present. 'Man', by contrast, unshackled from this 'vegetation of life', could act with consistency and endurance in the wider world. Whereas menstruation produced profound alterations in emotional state, its 'male equivalent', ejaculation, produced only 'a fleeting change of mood' (*flüchtige Gemütsänderung*).[30]

Against the background of this highly polarized model of

Karl Rosenkranz, Professor of Philosophy at the University of Königsberg. Engraving, 1860.

gender relations, Ebel was a disturbing presence. He was gentle and quietly spoken, with fine features and slender fingers. Contemporaries reported, as we have seen, that he appeared effeminate, that he wore his long hair 'like a lady'. Count Finckenstein described him as a 'hermaphrodite', attractive only to women and other girlish men like himself.[31] Among the stories that circulated about Ebel in the press was one that stemmed from Ludwig Wilhelm Sachs. It described an episode that had taken place during summer in the early 1820s. Sachs recalled that Ebel had contracted a 'repellent skin disease' and lived for some months in a village near a lake where he could bathe regularly, 'surrounded by many female *Mucker*'. One day his doctor (Sachs) came to visit him and was told that he was bathing in the lake. He went there and found that the men's bathing area was empty, but the women's was not. He became suspicious and went there to investigate. A half-dressed lady approached him and asked him not to come any nearer and disturb them, because 'Ebel is just now being washed by the ladies'. 'And sure enough, ten or twelve younger and older women had gone with this man into the lake and were vying with each other to irrigate the saint.' The inconsequentiality of this story is itself a clue to its importance. This wasn't a scene suggesting depravity; what captured the imagination of contemporaries was the presence of a man in a ladies' bathing enclosure.

Ebel was married with three children, but the queerness of his persona may be a clue to the events that unfolded around him. It may well explain his striking appeal to the women of his congregation, who saw in him an empathetic and unthreatening confidant. It may help to explain the unpatriarchal tone of the circle that gathered around him. That at least some male contemporaries saw the sociability of his circle as an assault on the patriarchal order is suggested by the claim that Ebel's 'sect' was tearing apart the great families of the region and luring women away from their husbands. In his reflections on sexual difference, Karl Rosenkranz noted that a small minority of persons existed who did not fall within the binary male–female schema; these were the 'hermaphrodites' and 'sissies' (*Weiblinge*) who crossed the divide – such people were well equipped to 'lead the machinations of intrigues and conspiracies' but could never be heroes or the pivot of events.[32] Viewed through the lens of this highly polarized understanding of gender relations, the predations of Sachs, von Hake and others of their ilk were peccadillos that, though vexatious and regrettable, ultimately affirmed the order in which they took place. By contrast, the Ebel of anti-Ebelian narrative resembled the androgynous god Dionysus, disturbingly attractive to women and even to some men, whose erotic cult threatened the civic order of ancient Thebes.

Hostile observers described the group as a women's church (*Frauenkirche*), macabrely attractive to 'women and effeminate males' (*männliche Zwitterwesen*).³³ It was notable that women were in a number of prominent cases assigned direct moral authority over men. It was believed that their teachings assigned women a 'great role as co-creator and instrument of divine power'.³⁴ Coupled with this was a distinctive emphasis on the importance of reciprocity in marriage, the effort to cultivate an open and frank relationship with sexuality (if only to diminish its power over the psyche), and the cultivation of a joyful and unforced form of sociability among the adherents, a sociability that did not exclude quite intimate platonic relations between men and women. Only through Ebel's sermons, Ida von der Groeben reported, did she become aware for the first time that Christianity can serve every need, including the needs of the intellect, and that this was 'the religion of awareness and therefore also of joy'. She had learned, moreover, that 'Christians were not servants, but rather children, volunteers, friends of God'. And the preacher – here she touched on the core of Ebel's style as a pastor and teacher – 'was not the lord over the faith of his congregation, but rather the helpers of their joy [*Gehülfe ihrer Freude*]'.³⁵

Many contemporary testimonies in support of Ebel touch on this notion of happiness. It was fun to be around Ebel – at least for women like Ida von der Groeben, and she was not the only one of whom it was said that Ebel's preaching and pastoral advice had awakened them from years of melancholy, rendering them capable of taking pleasure in everyday life. It was precisely the fact that women from the best families of the city had been encouraged to rethink their marital relationships, that prominent single women had been delighted and satisfied by the relationships they had forged within the circle, that these women had vouchsafed to Ebel a trust that they denied their husbands and male kinsmen, that enraged the men of the city's elite.

★

Closing Thoughts

In the winter season of 1839–40, Berliners flocked to the latest play by the dramatist, librettist and composer Carl Blum. In *Schwärmerei nach der Mode (Fashionable Fanatics)* a conniving and hypocritical clergyman by the name of Reckum has managed to attach himself to the wealthy Countess Angelika. She is the young widow of a man fallen some years ago on the field of battle, and is still grieving for her late husband – indeed she has made something of a cult out of her bereavement, which she refers to constantly. Her chief comfort is the oily and solicitous Dr Reckum, who beguiles her with fond touches, chaste kisses and pious incantations. Reckum's psychological hold on the countess – whose own mental health is fragile – is complete. In an unguarded moment, Reckum opens up to another character about his modus operandi:

> . . . coincidence brought me into the vicinity of a very respectable and wealthy lady. A new world opened up to me in new forms. I turned from the old road into a new and soon found my feet. I liked the luxurious, quiet, peaceful rooms; wherever the eye looked, it found balance and niceness; [. . .] the plentiful resources, excellent food, a comfortable apartment as a reward for my erudition, all had the effect of making me truly fond of my lady. [. . .] I became fashionable in her evening circle . . .

When a handsome suitor turns up and wins Angelika's heart, the grip of the parasitic Reckum is broken and he departs in disgrace, never to return.

This was a grossly crudified version of the *Mucker* narrative, in which the characters were flattened into cartoonish parodies. But anyone with even a passing familiarity with the Königsberg events could see the parallels. Reckum, whose name is

Playbill for the performance of *Schwarmerei nach der Mode* (*Fashionable Fanatics*) at the Hamburger Stadttheater, 27 July 1840. The women in the story largely disappeared from Carl Blum's retelling: 'Countess Angelika' is the only female role. Note that dance interludes follow the second and last act, a typical feature of the popular entertainments of the period.

Mucker in reverse, is not just the countess's spiritual adviser, he also leads a circle of devotees composed of notorious reformed sinners; he advises various characters to thwart the designs of Lucifer with the power of 'the seraph' – a play on the 'seraphic' delights supposedly enjoyed by the Ebelians in Königsberg.[36] Blum later recalled meeting Frederick William III leaving his box after one performance; the monarch waved him over and said: 'You have written a very entertaining piece; it went down well, but I think it will make you many enemies.'[37]

Schwärmerei nach der Mode swept across the German theatres, playing in Bremen, Hamburg, Weimar, Leipzig, Dresden, Königsberg and many other cities. The liberal diarist Carl Varnhagen von Ense saw it in Berlin and rightly judged it to be a 'badly constructed and badly filled-out piece, boring and silly'. Yet seeing it staged was an experience full of 'tension and excitement' because of the extraordinary public response. The house was full to bursting and the applause was deafening. On the night when Varnhagen attended, the king and various members of the Prussian royal family were watching from their boxes. At the sight of the religious phoney Dr Reckum, a shudder of delight passed through the audience. There was a sense that the play was an important reflection on the present moment; it was as if the topic mattered more than the specifics of what happened among the characters in the drama.[38] Friedrich Engels, who saw the play in Bremen in July 1840, was irritated by it. He mocked the claim, put out by 'many journals', that the play was 'timely'. It was true – here Engels agreed with Varnhagen – that *Schwärmerei nach der Mode* had done 'useful' service in putting the phenomenon of evangelical religious zeal onto the stage for the first time. But he argued that Blum's caricature of revivalist religion as a cover for 'deception, greed or refined sensuality' completely failed to do justice to the sincerity and moral seriousness that gave rise to excessive manifestations of religious feeling – the sign of a sensibility that reflected his own upbringing in pietist Elberfeld.[39] We can only imagine what it meant for Ebel, now in confinement, whose appeal against the first sentence was still pending, to be aped in this way in the theatre of his home town.

In retrospect, it is the vehemence of the public attacks on Ebel and Diestel that commands our attention. The motivations varied: the Ebelians believed that professional envy roused the clergymen of Königsberg against their successful and gifted colleague. They argued that authentic Christianity had always made enemies and that the fervent hostility of the foremost accusers was rooted in the failure of flawed individuals to live up to the stringent moral code of Ebel's circle. Government and church officials in Königsberg and Berlin were irritated by the fuss and keen to suppress and discourage all forms of separatist religion – for them, the *Mucker* were the shock troops of neo-pietist sectarianism.[40] The male, liberal intelligentsia of the city winced at the unusual emotional tone of the *Mucker* gatherings and the prominence assigned to women within them. And in the press coverage, which often emphasized the presence of 'high-born' persons among the *Mucker*, we also find a strain of bourgeois anti-nobiliary animus: the excesses of the zealots were taken to exemplify the corporate vices of a ruling class whose privileges and leadership role were, by implication, obsolete in a modern society.[41] These were not mutually exclusive views of the issue; on the contrary, they probably worked together and in parallel. When the feebleness of one line of attack was exposed, people could switch momentarily to another.

Whatever their motivations, the enemies of the *Mucker* sought an unconditional victory over the recalcitrant clergymen: their reputations were to be ruined; they must be removed from public life. 'When you have caught an eel,' Dr Sachs remarked at the end of his deposition to the Consistory, 'and you want to strip its skin, it is a good idea to hammer a nail through its head. I think I have made my meaning clear.'[42] Yet when the scandal was over, the emotion dissipated almost immediately. The attackers relaxed and moved on.[43] Reason had triumphed, there was nothing more to say. For those who admired, loved, or supported Ebel, by contrast, the sense of injustice and grievance was lasting. Its energy reverberates in the printed sources generated by the scandal.[44]

In her memoirs, Fanny Lewald reflected on the mechanism by which rumours and real-world observations fused into an apparently irrefutable reality: she observed that as the stories of sexual excess accumulated, people began to connect up things in new ways. They began to notice that the *Mucker* were perhaps paler and physically slighter than their non-*Mucker* contemporaries; their women seemed to have longer and thinner necks; one had to admit that the *Mucker* girls looked tired and wilted. The accumulated familiarity of people well known across the city retreated behind this new reality. People who had known each other well became mutually unintelligible.

It is not uncommon for historical narratives to be powered by a sense of right contending with wrong. To make this structure work, complex interactions have sometimes been reduced to confrontations between opposed historical principles: progress and reaction; light and darkness, reason and superstition. But the great sadness of the Ebel–Diestel scandal, Fanny Lewald remembered, lay precisely in the fact that it failed to play out in this way. She had a ringside view of the trial, at least indirectly: Ludwig Crelinger, the defender of Ebel and Diestel, lodged in her house, and the family of her best friend Mathilde were all *Mucker*. As a young girl and adolescent, Fanny had loved her teacher Johann Ebel and nothing had happened since then to diminish her esteem for him. She watched as good people were sucked into the maelstrom of the scandal; she was moved by reports of *Mucker* women steadfastly defending themselves against impertinent and deeply offensive lines of questioning.

The functionaries and publicists who oversaw the destruction of Ebel and Diestel were also people of quality. They viewed themselves as the carriers of a progressive world view. Theodor von Schön, the most important persecutor, is rightly admired as a reformer and a critic of the Berlin police state. We see in him one of the luminaries of early nineteenth-century German liberalism. The whole province, one liberal newspaper eulogized after his death in 1856, had revered him as a 'man of light'.[45] The theologians and publicists who laughed at Schönherr's cosmogony, the Fichtean minister Altenstein, who strove to remain equidistant from the extremes in politics and religion – they and others like them were exponents of the humane power of reason, who felt themselves to be on the right side of history. But reason could be a strict mistress, a tyrannical one even, when her champions sought in her name to impose on the supposedly incorrigible a better way of thinking and living. The light was not always on their side and their opponents were not always immersed in darkness.

*

[*1851: the writer Fanny Lewald, who is visiting Königsberg, and the philosopher Karl Rosenkranz meet by chance in a bookshop* on the Langgasse. Rosenkranz peers over her shoulder at the book she has taken from the shelf.]

'Is that the same Crelinger who defended the Mucker ten years ago?'

Lewald looks up. 'Herr Rosenkranz, what a pleasure. Yes, this is our Crelinger.' She shows him the volume.

Rosenkranz puts on his spectacles and reads out the title: *'Defence and Findings in the Case of the Bookseller Theile in Königsberg: A Contribution to the Theory of Insults and to the Appraisal of the Position of a Publisher in the case of Insulting Censored Publications.* Sounds dull! A far cry from our *"Mucker* trial" . . .'

'Not really.' Lewald replaces the book on the shelf. 'The trial of Ebel and Diestel opened with a defamation suit, remember?'

'So it did, now that you mention it. Finck contra Diestel. What an extraordinary time that was! Remember the summer of 1836, when the "Ebelians" were the subject of every conversation at every table? That was before the revolution – it seems like a century ago now. But I do recall one day in particular: I had gone for a long walk in the woods outside the city and came back to find bags of files on the desk in my study. There were letters with a request from the court and from the Dean of my Faculty that I write an expert opinion on the speculative content of the Ebel doctrine. And next to them, a massive cache of documents: letters to and from Ebel, conduct reports, depositions, the notes taken by students on his lectures and sermons, and so on. I was supposed to come to a judgement as to whether the beliefs expounded by Ebel and his associates were compliant with the "laws of thought and of physical nature" and even to what extent their principles were likely to have "immoral consequences". Can you imagine? I have to admit that I was very excited when I found my hands full of letters written in the greatest confidence by people I had never met. Not bad for an interloper from far-off Magdeburg. What would some of these Königsbergers not have given to be in my place!'

'Our friend Crelinger – he was lodging at my house during the trial – was not at all impressed by your "expert opinion".' She laughs. 'It arrived too late to be included with the original documentation, remember, and had to be added later by special allowance and sent by post to Berlin.'

'Well, that's true, but if they wanted a quick response, they shouldn't have sent me such a mountain of files!'

'It wasn't the timing that worried Crelinger, Herr Rosenkranz, it was the partisanship of the report itself.'

'My dear Fanny Lewald, if you mean by partisanship that I took the side of reason against zealotry, then I plead guilty! Look at this poor Ebel! He was the follower of Schönherr, a man who claimed to be the incarnation of the Holy Spirit, the proclaimer of the last Gospel . . . Ebel was far better educated than Schönherr, but he was a complete layman in the area of natural sciences. And then, armed with poorly understood readings of obscure tracts from the school of Schelling, he made himself ever less able to acquire a true understanding of nature and gradually dreamed himself into a similar sense of infallibility.'

'According to Crelinger, what your report lacked was *independence*. It was too beholden to the testimony of Ebel's enemies. You were so close to Provincial President von Schön, who was no friend of the accused. Wasn't it he' – she is teasing him now – 'who proposed you for this task? I am only saying this my dear Mr Rosenkranz because I actually knew Ebel quite well. I had known him since I was a little girl when he taught at my school. I never once saw him put on airs of infallibility. He was a dreamer, yes, perhaps, but he was the soul of gentleness and modesty.'

'Well, of course, you are quite right, Miss Lewald! We shouldn't forget that people of fine feelings, full of passion for the highest things, found their morality, their path to holiness in their connection with this gifted man.'

'Women in particular . . .'

'Yes! Intelligent, courageous but romantically overwrought women. Thanks to their high position in society, to their wealth, to their genuine religious need, they gradually worked their way to the point where they were the rulers of this society . . .'

'They didn't have to "work their way", Mr Rosenkranz – Ebel felt an affinity with these women, he listened to them, he assigned to them a certain creative authority.'

'Well yes, indeed! And if you put all of this together you will see that we have before us one of the most interesting phenomena of church history. It captures and exemplifies everything that was always there: from gnostic theogonies and allegorical interpretations of scripture to outlandish mixtures of the sensual and the spiritual, glowing devotion to one's convictions and the cunning discipline of secret societies.'

'These are fine words for the lecture hall, Mr Rosenkranz. But the characters caught up in all that commotion were not historical or allegorical exemplars, they were people.'

'I have never denied it!' interjects Rosenkranz.

Fanny Lewald continues: 'And they were good people. I remember one older lady – a well-known *Mucker* from an ancient family. She employed a local woman in her house whose face was disfigured by a horrific cancer – one could scarcely bring oneself to look at it; the poor creature could find work nowhere else. I often saw them talking quietly together and this lady never betrayed the slightest sign of disgust. It was as if she looked through the face at the person behind it. These are the people we are talking about.'

'Miss Lewald, I have never denied that there were good people among them . . .'

She cuts him off. 'One of them was my childhood best friend Mathilde. Her family were deeply embroiled in the controversy – on Ebel's side – and people urged my father to forbid me to see her. His sense of justice prevailed and Mathilde and I continued to meet, even if we could no longer be as close as before. Mathilde kept her distance from the investigation. She was as sweet-tempered and as true as ever. It goes without saying that she had no ability whatsoever even to imagine the enormities trafficked in the rumour mills of the press. But her soul darkened at the sight of what the controversy was doing to the people around her. When the man she loved, her betrothed, insisted that she break off all contact with the Ebel congregation, she stuck by them and resolved to separate from him. But my goodness, she suffered!'

Rosenkranz interjects: 'I can well imagine it.'

Fanny Lewald: 'Mathilde never complained – she said that true Christians had always been persecuted in this way. We still lived alongside each other. We still met and spoke often. But now a world had become between us, we understood each other less and less. That, Mr Rosenkranz, is the real moral of the story. The failure of understanding. Even as we sat in my room chatting in our accustomed spot, my childhood friend and I were already dead and buried for each other.'[46]

Notes

Chapter 1: The City of Almost

1 Ludwig von Baczko, *Versuch einer Geschichte und Beschreibung der Stadt Königsberg* (siebentes Heft, Königsberg, 1790), p. 106.
2 Fred J. Howlett and Nebraska Alpha, 'Königsberg Bridge Problem', *Pi Mu Epsilon Journal*, 3/5 (1961), pp. 218–23; Lydle Brinkle and Paul Griesacker, 'Euler's Solution (or Discoveries) in Relation to the Problem of the Königsberg Bridges: The Origin of the Mathematics of Topology', *Journal of the Pennsylvania Academy of Science*, 64/2 (1990), pp. 103–7.
3 Carl Johannes Fuchs and Georg Neuhaus, *Die Gemeindebetriebe der Stadt Königsberg i. Pr* (= Schriften des Vereins für Socialpolitik, vol. 129, part 9) *Gemeindebetriebe: Neue Versuche und Erfahrungen über die Ausdehnung der kommunalen Tätigkeit in Deutschland und im Ausland* (Berlin, 1910), pp. 2–3.
4 Cited in Bernd von Münchow-Pohl, *Zwischen Reform und Krieg. Untersuchungen zur Bewusstseinslage in Preussen, 1809–1812* (Göttingen, 1987), pp. 352–6.
5 Johann Theodor Schmidt, 'Ostpreußens Schicksale im Jahre 1812 während des Krieges zwischen Frankreich und Russland', in Karl-Gottfried Hagen (ed.), *Beiträge zur Kunde Preußens*, vol. 7 (Königsberg, 1825), pp. 1–51, 97–149, 185–258, 279–335, 379–414, here p. 391.
6 Report from Schön, 21 December 1812, cited in Münchow-Pohl, *Zwischen Reform und Krieg*, p. 378.

Notes

7 Schmidt, 'Ostpreußens Schicksale im Jahre 1812 während des Krieges zwischen Frankreich und Russland', pp. 396–7.
8 Karl Faber, *Die Haupt- und Residenz-Stadt Königsberg in Preußen. Das Merkwürdigste aus der Geschichte, Beschreibung und Chronik der Stadt* (Königsberg, 1840), p. 10.
9 Baczko, *Versuch einer Geschichte* (zweites Heft, Königsberg, 1788), p. 133.
10 Ibid. (drittes Heft, Königsberg, 1789), p. 251.
11 Fritz Gause, *Die Geschichte der Stadt Königsberg in Preussen*, 3 vols. (Cologne, 1968), vol. 2, *Von der Königskrönung bis zum Ausbruch des Ersten Weltkrieges*, p. 413.
12 Baczko, *Versuch einer Geschichte* (drittes Heft, Königsberg, 1789), p. 251.
13 Ibid., pp. 253–6.
14 Beata Wacławik, 'Das Archiv der Albertus-Universität Königsberg im Bestand des Staatsarchivs in Olsztyn (Allenstein)', *Biuletyn Polskiej Misji Historycznej*, 6 (2011), pp. 91–107, here p. 94; Gause, *Die Geschichte der Stadt Königsberg*, vol. 2, pp. 489–90.
15 Karl Rosenkranz, *Königsberger Skizzen* (Danzig, 1842), p. 65.
16 Fanny Lewald, *Meine Lebensgeschichte*, 2 vols. (Berlin, 1861 and 1862), vol. 2, *Leidensjahre*, p. 214.

Chapter 2: News from Königsberg

1 Schön to Altenstein (Minister for Church Affairs), Königsberg, 7 August 1835, GStA Berlin, HA I, Rep. 76 III, Sekt. 2, Abt. XVI, Nr. 4, Vol. 1, fols. 1–4.
2 On the history of the ministry, see Christina Rathgeber, 'Das Kultusministerium und die Kirchenpolitik 1817–1934', in: Wolfgang Neugebauer (ed.), *Das Kultusministerium auf seinen Wirkungsfeldern Schule, Wissenschaft, Kirchen, Künste und Medizinalwesen:*

Darstellung (Berlin, 2010), pp. 289–398; Bärbel Holtz, Rainer Paetau, Christina Rathgeber, Hartwin Spenkuch and Reinhold Zilch, *Das preußische Kultusministerium als Staatsbehörde und gesellschaftliche Agentur (1817–1934)*, vol. 1.1: *Die Behörde und ihr höheres Personal: Darstellung* (Berlin, 2009). These volumes form part of a series published by the Berlin-Brandenburgische Akademie der Wissenschaften: Wolfgang Neugebauer (ed.), *Preussen als Kulturstaat*, 13 vols. (Berlin, 2009–19).

3 Herbert Hömig, *Altenstein. Der erste preußische Kultusminister. Eine Biografie* (Münster, 2015), pp. 35, 36, 37.

4 The text of the Memorandum, in which the principal author, Karl August von Hardenberg, acknowledges the role played by Altenstein, can be consulted at: https://www.staatskanzler-hardenberg.de/quellentexte_riga.html. Altenstein composed a draft memorandum, which Hardenberg presented to the monarch along with his own; see Georg Winter, *Die Reorganisation des Preußischen Staates unter Stein und Hardenberg. Erster Teil: Allgemeine Verwaltungs- und Behördenreform, Band I: Vom Beginn des Kampfes gegen die Kabinettsregierung bis zum Wiedereintritt des Ministers vom Stein* (=Publikationen aus den Preußischen Staatsarchiven 93; Leipzig, 1931), p. 403. See also Hans Haußherr, 'Hardenberg's Reformdenkschrift, Riga 1807', *Historische Zeitschrift*, 157/2 (1938), pp. 267–308; Matthias A. Deuschle, 'Erweckung und Politik. Zur preußischen Religionspolitik unter Friedrich Wilhelm III.', *Zeitschrift für Theologie und Kirche*, 106/1 (2009), pp. 79–117, esp. p. 83.

5 Cited in Hömig, *Altenstein*, p. 75.

6 Ibid., pp. 21, 22, 178.

7 Cited in ibid., pp. 162, 144.

8 Ibid., p. 224; Deuschle, 'Erweckung und Politik', pp. 81–4.

9 Schön to Altenstein (Minister of Church Affairs), Königsberg, 7 August 1835, GStA Berlin, HA I, Rep. 76 III, Sekt. 2, Abt. XVI, Nr. 4, Vol. 1, fol. 1.

Notes

10 Ibid.
11 Ibid.
12 Ibid., fol. 3.
13 Ibid., fol. 4.
14 Christopher Clark, 'The Napoleonic Moment in Prussian Church Policy', in David Laven and Lucy Riall (eds.), *Napoleon's Legacy: Problems of Government in Restoration Europe* (Oxford, 2000), pp. 217–35, here p. 223; Christopher Clark, 'Confessional Policy and the Limits of State Action: Frederick William III and the Prussian Church Union 1817–1840', *Historical Journal*, 39 (1996), pp. 985–1004.
15 E.L. v. Gerlach, *Ernst Ludwig von Gerlach. Aufzeichnungen aus seinem Leben und Wirken 1795–1877*, ed. J. von Gerlach (Schwerin, 1903), pp. 132, 149–50.
16 Friedrich Wiegand, 'Eine Schwärmerbewegung in Hinterpommern vor hundert Jahren', *Deutsche Rundschau*, 189 (1921), pp. 323–36, here p. 333.
17 On sectarian activity in Masurian East Prussia as the expression of unmet religious needs, see Andreas Kossert, *Preußen, Deutsche oder Polen? Die Masuren im Spannungsfeld des ethnischen Nationalismus, 1870–1956* (Wiesbaden, 2001), p. 32.
18 See for example GStA Berlin, HA I, Rep. 76 III, Sekt. 1, Abt. XIIIa, Nr. 5, Vol. 1.

Chapter 3: The Prophet of the Pregel

1 Hermann Olshausen, *Lehre und Leben des Königsberger Theosophen Joh. Heinrich Schönherr* (Leipzig, 1838), pp. 24–9.
2 Ibid.
3 For a detailed official summary of Schönherr's hypothesis, see GStA Berlin, HA I, Rep. 76 III, Sekt. 2, Abt. XVI, Nr. 4b:

'Erkenntnis 1ster Instanz in der Untersuchungssache wider den Archidiakonus Dr Ebel und den Prediger Diestel in Königsberg Pr; eingereicht mittels Schreibens des Königlichen Kammergerichts hierselbst vom 15. August 1839', fols. 19–26.

4   Olshausen, *Lehre und Leben des Königsberger Theosophen*, pp. 12–13.

5   Immanuel Kant, *Critique of Pure Reason*, trans. J.M.D. Meiklejohn (London, 1890), p. xxix. On the importance to Kant more generally of momentary insight as a driver of transformative intellectual change, see Richard Bourke, *Hegel's World Revolutions* (Princeton, 2023), pp. 50–1.

6   Gottfried Wilhelm Herder, *Ideas for the Philosophy of the History of Mankind*, ed. and trans. Gregory Martin Moore (Princeton, 2024), Part One, Preface, p. 6. This treatise initially appeared under the title *Ideen zur Philosophie der Geschichte der Menschheit* in four separate volumes published in 1784, 1785, 1787 and 1791 respectively.

7   Friedrich Wilhelm Joseph Schelling, *Von der Weltseele, eine Hypothese der höheren Physik zur Erklärung des allgemeinen Organismus* [1798], 2nd edn (Hamburg, 1806), p. xlvi.

8   Johann Heinrich Diestel, Statement to the Consistorium, Königsberg, 15 October 1835, GStA Berlin, HA I, Rep. 76 III, Sekt. 2, Abt. XVI, Nr. 4, Vol. 1, fols. 60–96 verso.

9   William Hepworth Dixon, *Spiritual Wives* (London, 1868), p. 88.

10 Eduard von Hahnenfeld, *Die religiöse Bewegung zu Königsberg in Preußen in der ersten Hälfte des neunzehnten Jahrhunderts und die heutige Kirchengeschichte beleuchtet aus den von Wegnerschen "Mittheilungen" und ihren "authentischen Urkunden"* (Braunsberg, 1858), pp. 29, 31, 38, 44–5.

11 Thus the argument advanced by the experts engaged by the court to summarize the Schönherr 'doctrine', see GStA Berlin, HA I, Rep. 76 III, Sekt. 2, Abt. XVI, Nr. 4b: 'Erkenntnis 1ster Instanz', fol. 18.

12 Olshausen, *Lehre und Leben des Königsberger Theosophen*, pp. 24–9.

13 Ibid., pp. 15–16; Dixon, *Spiritual Wives*, p. 122.
14 Ida, Gräfin von der Gröben, geboren von Auerswald, *Die Liebe zur Wahrheit. Andeutungen* (Stuttgart, 1850), pp. 43, 51.
15 Gause, *Die Geschichte der Stadt Königsberg*, vol. 2, pp. 442–3.
16 'Die im Bezirk der Regierung zu Königsberg in Preußen befindlichen Vereine zu ausserkirchlichen Religionsübungen oder Erbauungsstunden zu 1822', GStA Berlin, HA I, Rep. 76 III, Sekt. 2, Abt. XVI, Nr. 1, Vol. 1, fols. 30–5.
17 For information on the Ebels as a pastoral family and on the importance of the Masurian regional context, I am grateful to Andreas Kossert, who discusses these matters in his *Preußen, Deutsche oder Polen? Die Masuren im Spannungsfeld des ethnischen Nationalismus 1870–1956* (Wiesbaden, 2001), esp. pp. 30–42.
18 Ernst, Graf von Kanitz, *Aufklärung nach Acten-Quellen über 1835 bis 1842 zu Königsberg in Preußen geführten Religionsprozeß für Welt- und Kirchengeschichte* (Basel und Ludwigsburg, 1862), p. 4.
19 Ibid.
20 Hahnenfeld, *Die religiöse Bewegung zu Königsberg*, p. i.
21 Dixon, *Spiritual Wives*, p. 108.
22 Fanny Lewald, *Im Vaterlande*, 2 Parts (Berlin, 1861), Part 1, p. 232.

Chapter 4: Ida's Awakening

1 Ida, Gräfin von der Gröben, geboren von Auerswald, *Die Liebe zur Wahrheit. Andeutungen* (Stuttgart, 1850), pp. 34, 32.
2 Ibid., pp. 36–7.
3 Ibid., pp. 38, 41.
4 Ibid., p. 47.
5 Anon., *Beobachtungen und Erfahrungen über Melancholische, besonders über die Religiöse Melancholie, von einem Prediger am Zuchthause zu T.* (Leipzig, 1799), p. 12.

6 Ibid., pp. 12, 14, 16, 17, 23.
7 von der Gröben, *Die Liebe zur Wahrheit*, p. 48.
8 Wayne E. Oates, *Religious Factors in Mental Illness* (London, 1957), pp. 36–9.
9 Friedrich Bird, 'Über die religiöse Melancholie', *Zeitschrift für die Anthropologie*, 1/1 (1823), pp. 228–41, 240, cited in Ann Goldberg, *Sex, Religion and the Making of Modern Madness: The Eberbach Asylum and German Society, 1815–1849* (Oxford, 1999), p. 45.
10 von der Gröben, *Die Liebe zur Wahrheit*, p. 47.

Chapter 5: Varieties of Religious Understanding

1 This exchange is a fiction. The opinions expressed are extrapolated in part from passages in David Friedrich Strauss, *Das Leben Jesu kritisch bearbeitet* (Stuttgart, 1836).
2 Adolf Hausrath, *David Friedrich Strauss und die Theologie seiner Zeit* (Heidelberg, 1876), pp. 379–82.
3 On these events, see Erik Linstrum, 'Strauss's "Life of Jesus": Publication and the Politics of the German Public Sphere', *Journal of the History of Ideas*, 71/4 (October 2010), pp. 593–616; Marc H. Lerner, *A Laboratory of Liberty: The Transformation of Political Culture in Republican Switzerland, 1750–1848* (Leiden and Boston, 2012), esp. ch. 5, 'Popular Sovereignty in the Züriputsch', pp. 221–64.
4 John McManners, *The French Revolution and the Church* (London, 1969), pp. 38, 46.
5 T.C.W. Blanning, 'The Role of Religion in European Counter-Revolution', in Derek Beales and Geoffrey Best (eds.), *History, Society and the Churches* (Cambridge, 1985), pp. 195–214.
6 Mariano Barbato, 'A State, a Diplomat and a Transnational Church: The Multi-Layered Actorness of the Holy See', *Perspectives*, 21/2, *The Changing Role of Diplomacy in the 21st Century* (2013), pp. 27–48.

Notes

7 Alexander Grab, *Napoleon and the Transformation of Europe* (Basingstoke, 2003), pp. 48–9.
8 Alexander Grab, 'Army, State, and Society: Conscription and Desertion in Napoleonic Italy (1802–1814)', *Journal of Modern History*, 67/1 (1995), pp. 25–54, here p. 34.
9 Ann Goldberg, *Sex, Religion and the Making of Modern Madness: The Eberbach Asylum and German Society, 1815–1849* (Oxford, 1999), p. 39.
10 Gustav Blumröder, 'Ueber religiösen Trübsinn', in Johannes Baptista Friedreich and Gustav Blumröder (eds.), *Blätter für Psychiatrie*, Heft 1 (Erlangen, 1837), pp. 14–16.

Chapter 6: The Difficult Ascent of Johann Ebel

1 Cited in Kanitz, *Aufklärung nach Acten-Quellen*, p. 10. I follow Kanitz's narrative closely here because he drew on documents that are no longer extant.
2 Ibid., pp. 10, 11, 12, 13.
3 Cited in ibid., p. 15.
4 Ibid.

Chapter 7: The Ebelians

1 Ernst Wilhelm, Graf von Kanitz, *Ein Mahnwort zu Gunsten der Nachwelt an die historische Literatur der Gegenwart. Nebst einem Auszuge aus dem "Zeugenverhör" von Prediger Diestel* (Basel and Ludwigsburg, 1868), p. 113.
2 'Die im Bezirk der Regierung zu Königsberg in Preußen befindlichen Vereine zu ausserkirchlichen Religionsübungen oder

Erbauungsstunden zu 1822', GStA Berlin, HA I, Rep. 76 III, Sekt. 2, Abt. XVI, Nr. 1, Vol. 1, fols. 30–5.

3 Cited in Deuschle, 'Erweckung und Politik', p. 85.

4 Hömig, *Altenstein*, p. 224, argues that Kawerau was the principal target of the new policy; Deuschle argues that the initiative stemmed from Theodor von Schön and was in fact directed against Ebel and his circle, Deuschle, 'Erweckung und Politik', pp. 85–91.

5 Kanitz, *Aufklärung nach Acten-Quellen*, p. 45. This exchange was reported to Kanitz by Ida von der Groeben, who was present when it took place.

6 'Mucker', in: Jacob Grimm and Wilhelm Grimm (eds.), *Deutsches Wörterbuch*, vol. 12, col. 2615, consulted online at: https://woerterbuchnetz.de/?sigle=DWB&lemid=M07773; also Adelung (ed.), *Grammatisch-kritisches Wörterbuch der Hochdeutschen Mundart* (Leipzig, 1793), vol. 3, col. 300, consulted at: https://woerterbuchnetz.de/?sigle=Adelung&lemid=M02165

7 Schön to Altenstein (Minister for Church Affairs), Königsberg, 7 August 1835, GStA Berlin, HA I, Rep. 76 III, Sekt. 2, Abt. XVI, Nr. 4, Vol. 1, fol. 4. See also Theodor von Schön to Joseph von Eichendorff, Königsberg, 30 November 1835, in Wilhelm Kosch (ed.), *Briefe an Freiherrn Joseph von Eichendorff* (Regensburg, 1910), letter 60, pp. 128–33, in which Schön describes the two groups as rooted in the same 'disreputable principle' (p. 131) but differing on the question of how to translate it into practice.

8 Altenstein was pleased with this 'good and worthy' statement from Tholuck, see Hömig, *Altenstein*, p. 223.

9 Kanitz, *Aufklärung nach Acten-Quellen*, p. 51.

Notes

Chapter 8: Charge and Counter-Charge

1 Finckenstein to Mirbach, Königsberg 14 January 1835, GStA Berlin, HA I, Rep. 76 III, Sekt. 2, Abt. XVI, Nr. 4, Vol. 1, fols. 5–6.
2 Ibid.
3 Diestel to Finckenstein, Königsberg, 4 May 1835, GStA Berlin, HA I, Rep. 76 III, Sekt. 2, Abt. XVI, Nr. 4a, fols. 13–42, fol. 14.
4 Ibid., fols. 15, 16, 16 verso, 17.

Chapter 9: Building a Case

1 Bernd Sösemann, 'Wissenschaft und Politik. Eine Kritik der Ansichten und Urteile über Schöns Leben und Werk in zwei Jahrhunderten', in idem. (ed.), *Theodor von Schön. Untersuchungen zu Biographie und Historiographie* (Cologne, 1996), pp. 1–28, here p. 21.
2 Schön himself acknowledged this fault in a note written shortly before his death, see 'Allgemeine menschliche Schwächen und Fehler (F27)', no date [after 1854], in Bernd Sösemann (ed.), *Theodor von Schön. Persönliche Schriften. Die autobiographischen Fragmente* (Cologne, 2006), pp. 756–66, here p. 757.
3 Ida von der Gröben, 'Obschwebender Criminal-Untersuchung', excerpted in Kanitz, *Aufklärung nach Acten-Quellen*, p. 64.
4 Ibid., pp. 69–73.
5 Ludwig August Kähler, *Supernaturalismus und Rationalismus in ihrem gemeinschaftlichen Urprunge, ihrer Zwietracht und höheren Einheit. Ein Wort zur Beruhigung für alle, welche nicht Wissen of sie glaubend erkennen oder erkennend glauben* (Leipzig, 1818), p. 114, note *.
6 Ludwig August Kähler, *Philagathos: Andeutungen über das Reich des Guten: Ein Beitrag zur einfachen Verständigung über christlich-religiöse Wahrheit*, 2 vols. (Königsberg, 1823–4); Kanitz, *Aufklärung nach Acten-Quellen*, p. 62.

Notes

7 Here I follow closely the analysis of Kanitz, *Aufklärung nach Acten-Quellen*, which draws in part on the legal challenges composed by the defence advocate Ludwig Crelinger.

Chapter 10: *The Trial Begins*

1 Cited in Kanitz, *Aufklärung nach Acten-Quellen*, p. 91.
2 Ibid., pp. 93–4.
3 On Crelinger, see Lewald, *Meine Lebensgeschichte*, vol. 2, *Leidensjahre*, pp. 225–34. On his skill as an advocate and for points picked up from his written objections, see Kanitz, *Aufklärung nach Acten-Quellen*, pp. 313, 321–427, passim.
4 Ida von der Groeben to Altenstein, Königsberg, 18 October 1835, GStA Berlin, HA I, Rep. 76 III, Sekt. 2, Abt. XVI, Nr. 4, Vol. 1, fols. 38–44, here fol. 40.
5 Prince William of Prussia to Altenstein, Berlin, 28 October 1835, ibid., fol. 36.

Chapter 11: *Diestel Testifies*

1 Record of the Deposition by Diestel before the Consistorium in Königsberg, 15 October 1835, GStA Berlin, HA I, Rep. 76 III, Sekt. 2, Abt. XVI, Nr. 4, Vol. 1, fols. 54–9 verso, here fols. 54–54 verso.
2 Georg Heinrich Diestel, *Johann Heinrich Schönherr's Princip der beiden Urwesen als die nothwendige und abweisbare Grundlage wahrer Philosophie*, in Heinrich Diestel and Johann Ebel, *Verstand und Vernunft im Bunde mit der Offenbarung Gottes durch das Anerkenntnis des wörtlichen Inhalts der heiligen Schrift. Zwei Abhandlungen* (Leipzig, 1837), p. viii.

Notes

3   Diestel, Statement to the Consistorium, Königsberg, 15 October 1835, GStA Berlin, HA I, Rep. 76 III, Sekt. 2, Abt. XVI, Nr. 4, Vol. 1, fols. 60–96 verso, here fol. 67.
4   Consistorium, Königsberg, to MGUMA, Königsberg, 21 October 1835, GStA Berlin, HA I, Rep. 76 III, Sekt. 2, Abt. XVI, Nr. 4, Vol. 1, fols. 51–3.
5   'In der Schilderung ist eine Anweisung zu unnatürlicher Überreizung des Körpers gegeben, die ich verabscheuen muss, und nicht empfohlen haben kann', Diestel to Consistorium, 15 and 16 October 1835, GStA Berlin, HA I, Rep. 76 III, Sekt. 2, Abt. XVI, Nr. 4, Vol. 1, fols. 54–9, here fol. 56.
6   Hahnenfeld, *Die religiöse Bewegung zu Königsberg*, pp. 74, 78.
7   Deposition by Diestel before the Consistorium in Königsberg, 15 October 1835, GStA Berlin, HA I, Rep. 76 III, Sekt. 2, Abt. XVI, Nr. 4, Vol. 1, fols. 54–9 verso, here fols. 57, 58.
8   The letter from Wilhelmine von Finckenstein is transcribed in Diestel to Consistorium, 'Ausführliche Erklärung des Predigers Diestel über die dem Archidiakonus Dr. Ebel erkennbar gemachten Anschuldigungen', Königsberg, 15 Oktober 1835, GStA Berlin, HA I, Rep. 76 III, Sekt. 2, Abt. XVI, Nr. 4, Vol. 1, fols. 60–96; the letter is transcribed on fols. 81–4, here fol. 84.
9   This point is made in Diestel to Consistorium, ibid., here fol. 88.
10 Ralph Gibson, 'Why Republicans and Catholics Couldn't Stand Each Other in the Nineteenth Century', in Frank Tallett and Nicholas Atkin (eds.), *Religion, Society and Politics in France since 1789* (London, 1991), pp. 107–20.
11 Ebel to Ministry of Church Affairs, Königsberg, 12 October 1835, GStA Berlin, HA I, Rep. 76 III, Sekt. 2, Abt. XVI, Nr. 4, Vol. 1, fols. 23–5.

Notes

Chapter 12: A Media Sensation

1 Friedrich Wilhelm III to Rochow and Altenstein, Berlin, 26 April 1836, GStA Berlin, HA I, Rep. 76 III, Sekt. 2, Abt. XVI, Nr. 4, Vol. 1, fols. 236–8.
2 On student rowdiness, see Dixon, *Spiritual Wives*, pp. 27–31; on lampoons, see Schön to Altenstein, Königsberg, 28 September 1835, GStA Berlin, HA I, Rep. 76 III, Sekt. 2, Abt. XVI, Nr. 4, Vol. 1.
3 For example, the *Elbinger Anzeigen* ran a piece describing Ebel as a self-proclaimed 'new Messiah' on 27 September 1835; see also 'Zuverlässige Mittheilungen über Johann Heinrich Schönherrs Theosophie [. . .] sowie über die durch letztere Veranlaßten sectiererischen Umtriebe zu Königsberg in Preußen', *Illgens Zeitschrift für historische Theologie* (1838); reports attacking Ebel and his associates appeared in the *Evangelische Kirchenzeitung* of 1836; on the public resonance of the case, see Kanitz, *Aufklärung nach Acten-Quellen*, pp. 128–44.
4 *Staats- und Gelehrten-Zeitung des Hamburgischen Correspondenten*, Friday, 1 April 1836; transcribed in GStA Berlin, HA I, Rep. 76 III, Sekt. 2, Abt. XVI, Nr. 4, Vol. 1, fol. 231.
5 *Evangelische Kirchenzeitung*, 9 March 1836: 'Nachrichten. Erlangen, 28 February 1836', transcribed in GStA Berlin, HA I, Rep. 76 III, Sekt. 2, Abt. XVI, Nr. 4, Vol. 1, fol. 229.
6 'Neuestes Leben und Treiben auf unserem Planeten. Königsberg, Anfang Februar 1836', *Unser Planet. Blätter für Unterhaltung, Zeitgeschichte, Literatur, Kunst und Theater*, no. 70, Tuesday 22 March 1836, p. 275, cutting in HA 1 Rep. 76 III, Sekt 2. Abt. XVI, Nr. 4, Vol. 2.
7 Extrakt aus der *Kritischen Prediger-Bibliothek von Dr. Röhr*, 17/1 (1836), GStA Berlin, HA I, Rep. 76 III, Sekt. 2, Abt. XVI, Nr. 4, Vol. 1, fol. 238.

8 Ibid., fols. 237–8.
9 Christopher Clark, *The Politics of Conversion: Missionary Protestantism and the Jews in Prussia, 1728–1941* (Oxford, 1995), p. 138.
10 'Die im Bezirk der Regierung zu Königsberg in Preußen befindlichen Vereine zu ausserkirchlichen Religionsübungen oder Erbauungsstunden zu 1822', GStA Berlin, HA I, Rep. 76 III, Sekt. 2, Abt. XVI, Nr. 1, Vol. 1, fols. 30–5; on gendered and sexual themes in anti-Catholic discourse during the Culture Wars, see Michael B. Gross, *The War against Catholicism: Liberalism and the Anti-Catholic Imagination in Nineteenth-Century Germany* (Ann Arbor, 2004); Manuel Borutta, *Antikaholizismus. Deutschland und Italien im Zeitalter der europäischen Kulturkämpfe* (Göttingen, 2010).
11 'Unus pro multis' [pseud., trans: One for Many], 'An die Mucker, eine neue religiöse (?) Secte im Preußenlande' [my translation], *Unser Planet. Blätter für Unterhaltung, Zeitgeschichte, Literatur, Kunst und Theater* 7 (1836), Nr. 47, 24 February 1836.
12 See, for example, ibid., Nr. 65, 16 March 1836; Nr. 69, 21 March 1836; Nr. 70, 22 March 1836; Nr. 82, 5 April 1836; Nr. 154, 28 June 1836; Nr. 183, 1 August 1836.
13 'Die Mucker', *Allgemeine Zeitung von und für Bayern: Tagsblatt für Politik, Literatur und Unterhaltung* 2, Nr. 272, 29 September 1835, and Nr. 273, 30 September 1835.
14 *Regensburger Zeitung*, Nr. 258, 29 October 1835.
15 *Augsburger Postzeitung. Ein Blatt statistisch-politischen Inhaltes*, Nr. 317, 13 November 1835.

Chapter 13: Dr Sachs Accuses

1 Christian Tilitzki, *Die Albertus-Universität Königsberg ihre Geschichte von der Reichsgründung bis zum Untergang der Provinz Ostpreußen*

Notes

  (1871–1945), 2 vols. (Berlin, 2012–13), Band 1 1871–1918, pp. 54–5; on Sachs's 'excitable temperament', which 'made him in early years a passionate supporter of Ebel' and the 'metaphysical ballast' that got in the way of his science, see Hans Prutz, *Die Königliche Albertus-Universität Königsberg i. Preußen im neunzehnten Jahrhundert zur Feier ihres 350-jährigen Bestehens* (Königsberg, 1894), p. 269.
2 Statement to the court by Sachs, Königsberg 15 July 1836, in Dixon, *Spiritual Wives*, vol. 2, pp. 295–344, here p. 298.
3 Fanny Lewald, *Im Vaterlande*, 2 Parts (Berlin, 1861), Part 2, p. 29.
4 Ludwig Wilhelm Sachs, *Über Wissen und Gewissen. Reden an Ärzte von Ludwig Wilhelm Sachs, der Medizin und Chirirgie Doctor, Professor der Medizin an der Universität zu Königsberg, Ritter des Vladimirordens vierten Klasse* (Berlin, 1826), p. ix.
5 Ibid., p. 4.
6 Ibid., p. 54.
7 Ibid., pp. 58–9.
8 Ibid., pp. 62–3, 65, 69, 71.
9 Sachs, Statement to the Court, Königsberg, 15 July 1836, pp. 295–344, transcribed in Dixon, *Spiritual Wives*, p. 296.
10 Ibid., pp. 297–8.
11 Kanitz, *Aufklärung nach Acten-Quellen*, pp. 282–3.
12 Ibid., p. 309.
13 Ibid., pp. 332, 334.
14 'Erkenntnis 1ster Instanz in der Untersuchungssache wider den Archidiakonus Dr Ebel und den Prediger Diestel in Königsberg Pr; eingereicht mittels Schreibens des Königlichen Kammergerichts hierselbst vom 15. August 1839', GStA Berlin, HA I, Rep. 76 III, Sekt. 2, Abt. XVI, Nr. 4b, unnumbered folios.
15 Ibid., unnumbered folios [132–3].
16 The volume in which these testimonies are excerpted is GStA Berlin, HA I, Rep. 76 III, Sekt. 2, Abt. XVI, Nr. 4b. The missing volume would have carried the number 4c in the same series.

Notes

I am extremely grateful to Stefanie Bellach of the Geheimes Staatsarchiv for her help in searching for the absent file.

17 Sachs, Statement to the Court, Königsberg, 15 July 1836, pp. 295–344, transcribed in Dixon, *Spiritual Wives*, p. 344.
18 'Erkenntnis 1ster Instanz', GStA Berlin, HA I, Rep. 76 III, Sekt. 2, Abt. XVI, Nr. 4b, unnumbered fols., fol. 128.
19 Ibid., fol. 129.

Chapter 14: The End of the Road

1 Altenstein to Consistorium, Königsberg, Berlin, 26 November 1835, GStA Berlin, HA I, Rep. 76 III, Sekt. 2, Abt. XVI, Nr. 4, Vol. 1, fol. 131.
2 Altenstein to Diestel, Berlin, 26 November 1835, Ibid., fols. 136–8.
3 Altenstein discusses this letter (of 22 June 1836), and the prosecution that resulted, in the ministerial memorandum 'Votum des Ministers der GUMA', Berlin 29 April 1837, ibid., Vol. 2, fols. 78–9. On the earlier sentence to three months in prison or a fine of 200 thalers, see Der Criminalsenat-des Oberlandesgerichts überreicht das [sic] Erkenntnis erster Instanz in der Untersuchungssache wider den hiesigen Prediger Johann Georg Heinrich Diestel, Königsberg, 4 September 1836, ibid., Vol. 2, fols. 2–25.
4 Widow Consentius geb. Lorck, to Altenstein, Königsberg, 12 October 1835, ibid., Vol. 1, fol. 28.
5 Carl Benjamin Waschke, Lehrer am Königlichen Waisenhause und Schullehrer-Seminar to Frederick William III, 15 December 1835, ibid., Vol. 1, fols. 145–6.
6 Tribunal-Rath Graf Kanitz to Consistorium, Königsberg, 10 November 1835, ibid., Vol. 1, fol. 188; Kanitz to Altenstein, Königsberg, 6 March 1836, ibid., Vol. 1, fols. 200–2.

7 Diestel to Oberlandesgericht, Königsberg, 8 December 1835, ibid., Vol. 1, fol. 149.
8 Diestel to MGUMA, Königsberg, 18 May 1836, ibid., Vol. 2, fol.
9 Petition from members of the Ebel congregation to Frederick William III (sent to Altenstein), Königsberg, 17 November 1835, ibid., Vol. 1, fols. 227–8.
10 'Members of the Old City Congregation and Listeners to Archdeacon Dr Ebel' to Frederick William III, Königsberg, 1 September 1836, ibid., Vol. 2, fols. 54–5.
11 'Erkenntnis 1ster Instanz in der Untersuchungssache wider den Archidiakonus Dr Ebel und den Prediger Diestel in Königsberg Pr; eingereicht mittels Schreibens des Königlichen Kammergerichts hierselbst vom 15. August 1839', GStA Berlin, HA I, Rep. 76 III, Sekt. 2, Abt. XVI, Nr. 4b, unnumbered folios.
12 Kanitz, *Aufklärung nach Acten-Quellen*, p. 321.
13 I draw here on the analysis in ibid., pp. 338–48.
14 Deposition by Ebel, transcribed in 'Erkenntnis 1ster Instanz', GStA Berlin, HA I, Rep. 76 III, Sekt. 2, Abt. XVI, Nr. 4b.
15 Paul Konschel, *Der Königsberger Religionsprozess gegen Ebel und Diestel (Muckerprozess)* (Königsberg, 1909), p. 106.
16 Lewald, *Leidensjahre*, p. 234.
17 Konschel, *Der Königsberger Religionsprozess*, p. 106.

Chapter 15: Closing Thoughts

1 'Allerlei', in *Allgemeine Zeitung von und für Bayern: Tagsblatt für Politik, Literatur und Unterhaltung* 2, no. 272, 29 September 1835.
2 Schön to Altenstein, Königsberg, 7 August 1835, GStA Berlin, Rep. 76 III, Sekt. 2, Abt. XVI, Nr. 4, Vol. 1, fol. 1; the same point is made in Finck von Finckenstein to Zelina von Mirbach, Königsberg, 14 January 1835, ibid., Vol. 1, fol. 6.

3 Rosenkranz, *Königsberger Skizzen*, p. 325.
4 Heinrich Diestel and Johann Ebel, *Verstand und Vernunft im Bunde mit der Offenbarung Gottes. Zwei Abhandlungen* (Leipzig, 1837), a leaflet based on a statement of belief composed by the two preachers at the request of the Consistorium; on this feature of Ebel's work, see also Kanitz, *Aufklärung nach Acten-Quellen*, pp. 4–5, 354.
5 Diestel, Statement to the Consistorium, Königsberg, 15 October 1835, GStA Berlin, HA I, Rep. 76 III, Sekt. 2, Abt. XVI, Nr. 4, Vol. 1, fol. 67.
6 Johann Heinrich Ebel, *Der Schlüssel zur Erkenntnis der Wahrheit in Entwickelung und offener Darlegung einer Ansicht über J.H. Schönherr's Ausschlüsse der Bibel und Natur-Offenbarung, Nebst einem Anhange fremder, jedoch verwandter Gedanken*, in Heinrich Diestel and Johann Ebel, *Verstand und Vernunft*, pp. 2, 3.
7 Ida von der Groeben to Minister Altenstein, Königberg, 18 October 1835, GStA Berlin, HA I, Rep. 76 III, Sekt. 2, Abt. XVI, Nr. 4, Vol. 1, fols. 38–44, here fol. 40.
8 Sachs, statement to the Court, Königsberg, 15 July 1836, in Dixon, *Spiritual Wives*, pp. 295–344, here p. 295.
9 Schön to Altenstein, Königsberg, 22 June 1836, GStA Berlin, HA I, Rep. 76 III, Sekt. 2, Abt. XVI, Nr. 4, Vol. 2, fol. 45.
10 Schön to Ida von der Groeben, 11 November 1835, transcribed in Kanitz, *Aufklärung nach Acten-Quellen*, pp. 286–7 (my italics).
11 Ida von der Groeben to Theodor von Schön, Königsberg, 18 October 1835, transcribed in ibid.
12 Eveline Ernestine von Bardeleben, *Ein Blick auf die einstige Stellung der Oberpräsidenten Auerswald und Schön in Königsberg und Preussen mit Rücksicht auf einige dahin bezügliche Schriften* (Stuttgart, 1844), pp. 47, 48, 50.
13 Graf Kanitz to Altenstein, Königsberg, 12 October 1835, GStA Berlin, HA I, Rep. 76 III, Sekt. 2, Abt. XVI, Nr. 4, Vol. 1, fols. 26–26a.

Notes

14 Herward Bork, *Zur Geschichte des Nationalitätenproblems in Preussen. Die Kirchenpolitik Theodors von Schön in Ost- und Westpreussen 1815–1843* (Leipzig, 1933), pp. 109–10.
15 Theodor von Schön to Altenstein, Königsberg, 6 March 1836, GStA Berlin, HA I, Rep. 76 III, Sekt. 2, Abt. XVI, Nr. 4, Vol. 1, fols. 200–23.
16 Ibid.
17 Cabinet Order from Frederick William III to Altenstein and von Rochow, Potsdam, 26 April 1836, ibid., Vol. 1, fols. 235–6.
18 Frederick William III to Ebel and Diestel, Potsdam, 26 April 1836, ibid., Vol. 2, fol. 42.
19 Schön to Altenstein (Minister of Church Affairs), Königsberg, 7 August 1835, ibid., Vol. 1, fols. 1–4.
20 Schön to Altenstein, Königsberg, 28 September 1835, ibid., Vol. 1, fol. 7.
21 Altenstein to Frederick William III, Berlin, 24 October 1835, ibid., Vol. 1, fols. 34–5.
22 Hahnenfeld, *Die religiöse Bewegung zu Königsberg*, p. 1.
23 Ibid., pp. 153, 154, 171, 177–80.
24 Wolfgang Neugebauer, 'Die preußischen Provinzialstände nach 1823/24 und Theodor von Schön', in Sösemann (ed.), *Theodor von Schön. Untersuchungen zu Biographie und Historiographie* (= Werner Vogel und Iselin Gundermann (eds.) Veröffentlichungen aus den Archiven Preußischer Kulturbesitz, Bd. 42) (Cologne, 1996), pp. 125–40, here p. 137.
25 Bardeleben, *Ein Blick auf die einstige Stellung*, p. 48.
26 Richard van Dülmen, *The Society of the Enlightenment: The Rise of the Middle Class and Enlightenment Culture in Germany*, trans. Anthony Williams (Oxford, 1992), pp. 47–8; Ferdinand Runkel, *Geschichte der Freimaurerei in Deutschland*, 3 vols. (Berlin, 1931–2), vol. 1, pp. 154–8.
27 Eduardo Mendieta, 'The Power of Religion in the Public Sphere', in idem. and Jonathan Van Antwerpen (eds.), *The Power of Religion*

in the Public Sphere (New York, 2011), pp. 1–14, here p. 2; Niamh Reilly, 'Introduction: Religion, Gender and the Public Sphere: Mapping the Terrain', in eadem. and Stacey Scriver (eds.), *Religion, Gender and Public Sphere* (London, 2014), pp. 1–17.

28 Lewald, *Leidensjahre*, pp. 218–19.
29 Karl Rosenkranz, *Aus einem Tagebuch. Königsberg Herbst 1833 bis Frühjahr 1846* (Leipzig, 1854), pp. 78–9.
30 Karl Rosenkranz, *Psychologie oder die Wissenschaft vom subjektiven Geist*, 3rd ed. (Königsberg, 1863 [1st ed. 1837]), pp. 100–1.
31 Finckenstein to Mirbach, Königsberg, 14 January 1835, GStA Berlin, HA I, Rep. 76 III, Sekt. 2, Abt. XVI, Nr. 4, Vol. 1, fols. 5–6.
32 Rosenkranz, *Psychologie oder die Wissenschaft vom subjektiven Geist*, p. 102.
33 On the supposed attractiveness of the group to women and 'effeminate males' (*männliche Zwitterwesen*), see Finckenstein to Zelina von Mirbach, Königsberg, 14 January 1835, transcribed in GStA Berlin, HA I, Rep. 76 III, Sekt. 2, Abt. XVI, Nr. 4, Vol. 1, fol. 6.
34 Lewald, *Leidensjahre*, p. 221.
35 Ida von der Groeben to Prince Wilhelm of Prussia, Königsberg, 18 October 1835, GStA Berlin, HA I, Rep. 76 III, Sekt. 2, Abt. XVI, Nr. 4, Vol. 1, fols. 38–44, here fol. 41. Emphasis in the original; the phrase relating to Ebel's pastorship is from 2 Corinthians 1:24: 'Not for that we have dominion over your faith but are helpers of your joy'; this was a stock theme in the sermons of the Awakened after 1815, see the inaugural sermon 'Der Diener des Evangeliums ist nicht Herr über euren Glauben sondern Gehülfe eurer Freude', held by the Awakened Elberfeld preacher Gottfried Daniel Krummacher on 11 February 1816, idem., *Gottfr. Dan. Krummacher's gute Botschaft in fünfundvierzig Predigten*, ed. Emil Wilhelm Krummacher (Elberfeld, 1838); on the same theme, see his brother, the reformed theologian Friedrich

Adolph Krummacher, *Die christliche Volkssschule im Bunde mit der Kirche* (Essen, 1825), p. 42.

36 Carl Blum, *Schwärmerei nach der Mode*, in idem., *Theater von Carl Blum*, 3 vols. (Berlin, 1844), pp. 1–116.

37 See the obituary for Carl Blum in L. Wolff, *Almanach für Freunde der Schauspielkunst auf das Jahr 1844* (Berlin, 1 January 1845), pp. 109–26, here p. 122.

38 Varnhagen von Ense, diary entry, Berlin, 6 January 1840, in idem., *Tagebücher von K.A. Varnhagen*, vol. 1 (Leipzig, 1861), pp. 160–1.

39 Friedrich Engels, 'Theatre: Publishing Festival', *Morgenblatt für gebildete Leser*, 181, 30 July 1840, consulted online at: https://www.marxists.org/archive/marx/works/1840/07/bremen.htm

40 Grzegorz Jasiński, 'Neopietizm a postawy narodowe. Ruch promadkarski na Masurach w XIX. I XX w. (do 1956). Część I', *Gdański Rocznik Evangelicki*, 8 (2014), pp. 108–34, here pp. 108–9.

41 See, for example, Regiomontanus [pseud., trans: Königsberger], 'Ausführlichster Bericht über die Mucker und ihr verworfenes Thun, mit reflectirenden Blicken nach allen Seiten, mit Beispielen und Parallelen', in *Unser Planet. Blätter für Unterhaltung, Zeitgeschichte, Literatur, Kunst und Theater*, 7 (1836), no. 65, 16 March 1836; no. 69, 21 March 1836; no. 70, 22 March 1836.

42 Cited in ibid., no. 70, 22 March 1836, p. 279.

43 In a note reflecting on his own weaknesses, written shortly before his death, Schön recalled the controversy over the trial of Ebel as one of the 'four occasions [on which] I have been publicly slandered' – see 'Allgemeine menschliche Schwächen und Fehler (F27)', no date [after 1854], in Sösemann (ed.), *Theodor von Schön. Persönliche Schriften*, p. 760.

44 See, for example, the anonymous article by 'Lawyer' in 'Blätter für literarische Unterhaltung', 1833, no. 170, p. 171; Johann Wilhelm Ebel and Georg Heinrich Diestel, *Zeugnis der Wahrheit. Zur Beseitigung der Olshausenschen Schrift: 'Lehre und Leben des Königsberger*

Theosophen Joh. Heinrich Schönherr' (Leipzig, 1838); Ernst von Hahnefeld, *Ein Moment aus den 'Mittheilungen' des Consistorialrath Kähler über das 'Leben und die Schriften' seines Vaters, beleuchtet von E. v. Hanhnefeld* (Braunsberg, 1856), a brochure defending Ebel and his mentor; Ernst von Hahnefeld, *Die religiöse Bewegung zu Königsberg in Preußen in der ersten Hälfte des neunzehnten Jahrhunderts und die heutige Kirchengeschichte* (Braunsberg, 1858); Ida von der Groeben, *Die Liebe zur Wahrheit* (Stuttgart, 1850); G.H. Diestel, *Ein Zeugenverhör im Criminalprozesse gegen die Prediger Eben und Diestel mit der darüber laut gewordenen Publicität angestellt* (Basel, 1868); E. v. Kanitz, *Aufklärung nach Actenquellen über den 1835 bis 1842 zu Königsberg in Preussen geführten Religionsprozess* (Basel, 1862); E.v. Kanitz, *Ein Mahnwort zu Gunsten der Nachwelt, an die historische Literatur der Gegenwart* (Basel, 1868).

45 Anon., 'Theodor von Schön', *Illustrierte Zeitung* (Leipzig), no. 687, 30 August 1856, cited in Sösemann, 'Wissenschaft und Politik', p. 1.

46 This dialogue is a fiction. The opinions expressed in it are extrapolated from Rosenkranz, *Königsberger Skizzen*, Karl Rosenkranz, *Aus einem Tagebuch. Königsberg Herbst 1833 bis Frühjahr 1846* (Leipzig, 1854), and Lewald, *Meine Lebensgeschichte*, vol. 2, *Leidensjahre*.

Acknowledgements

I am grateful to Stefanie Bellach of the Geheimes Staatsarchiv in Dahlem, Berlin, for advice on the files relating to the Ebel investigation and to Klaus Tempel, who has always made visits to this archive such a pleasure. Simon Winder of Penguin was as inspirational as ever and James Pullen of the Wylie Agency gave encouragement and sharp advice. Thanks to Richard Mason for his copy-editing and to Cecilia Mackay for help with the images. Special thanks are due to those who read and commented on versions of the manuscript: Ursula Dubosarsky, Jean-Michel Johnston, Deborah Lambie, James Mackenzie, Kristina Spohr, Charles Turner and Gero von Böhm. Michael Ledger-Lomas shared brilliant insights about the religious life of this period and Andreas Kossert helped me to situate the events in the confessional landscape of East Prussia. Marion Kant, who knows this period deeply, enriched the book with ideas and suggestions. We both miss my former doctoral supervisor Jonathan Steinberg, to whom this book is dedicated. It is inspired by two features of Jonathan's work as a teacher and writer: a feeling for how circumscribed transactions and episodes can illuminate larger problems, and a sensitivity to the place of personality and subjective perception in the dramas and conflicts that interest historians.

List of Illustrations and Photo Credits

Photographic acknowledgements are given in italics.

ENDPAPERS

Front: The Prussian States, detail of a map published by Justus Perthus, Gotha, 1833. *David Rumsey Map Collection.*

Rear: Königsberg, detail of a map published by Paul Schmidt, Berlin, 1809. *Provincial and Municipal Public Library, Bydgoszcz, Poland.*

ILLUSTRATIONS IN THE TEXT

p. 2. Bird's-eye plan of Königsberg. Engraving by Matthäus Merian, 1652. *Sunny Celeste / Alamy.*

p. 9. View of the Green Bridge over the Old Pregel River, Königsberg. Print published by W. Barth, c. 1810. *Wikimedia Commons.*

p. 14. Carl Freiherr vom Stein zum Altenstein. Lithograph by Emil Krafft, 1826. *Wikimedia Commons.*

p. 20. Frederick William III, King of Prussia. Engraving by A. Pflugfelder after a portrait by François Gérard, 1816. *Penta Springs / Alamy.*

p. 22. (Left) The Old Old City Church, Königsberg. Engraving, 1820; (right) The Haberberg Church. Photograph, late 19th century. *Bildarchiv Ostpreussen.*

List of Illustrations and Photo Credits

p. 32. The house of Immanuel Kant, Prinzessinstraße, Königsberg. Print by Friedrich Heinrich Bils, 1842. *Wikimedia Commons.*

p. 50. Confrontation on the Paradeplatz, Zürich, 6 September 1839. Print by J. W. Bachmann. *Zentralbibliothek, Zürich.*

p. 61. Altar of the Haberberg church. Photograph reproduced in Adolf Botticher, *Die Bau- und Kunstdenkmäler der Provinz Ostpreußen. Heft 7: Königsberg*, 1897.

p. 65. Title-page to Johann Wilhelm Ebel, *Die Apostoliche Predigt ist zeitgemäß*, 1835. *Bayerische Staatsbibliothek, Munich.*

p. 68. Heinrich Theodor von Schön, 1834. Engraving by A. Teichel after a drawing by J. Wolff. *akg-images.*

p. 88: Frederick William, Crown Prince of Prussia, 1835. Engraving by Auguste Hüssener after Franz Krüger. *Stiftung Stadtmuseum, Berlin / Dorin Ionita, 2021.*

p. 104: Fanny Lewald, 1848. Drawing by Wilhelm August Rudolf Lehmann. *Wikimedia Commons.*

p. 119. Petition from members of the Ebel congregation to King Frederick William III, 17 November 1835. *GStA Berlin, HA I, Rep. 76 III, Sekt. 2, Abt. XVI, Nr 4., Vol. 1, fols. 227–228.*

p. 120. Petition by 'Members of the Old City Congregation and Listeners to Archdeacon Dr Ebel' to King Frederick William III of Prussia, 14 September 1836. *GStA Berlin, HA I, Rep. 76 III, Sekt. 2, Abt. XVI, Nr 4., vol. 2, fols. 54–55.*

P. 138. Francisco da Goya, *El sueño de la razon produce monstruos*. Etching from the series, 'Los Caprichos', 1799. *Metropolitan Museum of Art, New York. Gift of M. Knoedler & Co., 1918.*

List of Illustrations and Photo Credits

p. 140. Karl Rosenkranz, Professor of Philosophy at the University of Königsberg. Engraving, 1860. *Private collection.*

p. 144. Playbill for the performance of *Schwarmerei nach der Mode* (*Fashionable Fanatics*) at the Hamburger Stadttheater, 27 July 1840. *Staats- und Universitätsbibliothek Hamburg Carl von Ossietzky, Hamburg. Photo courtesy of SUBHH Hamburg.*

Des Preussischen Staats östlicher Theil, oder OST- und WEST-PREUSSEN und POSEN.

entw. u. gez. v. A. Stieler 1819.

OSTSEE